a beginner's guide to digital video

ava

AVA Pub
Switzerl

An AVA Book
Published by AVA Publishing SA
c/o Fidinter SA
Ch. de la Joliette 2
Case postale 96
1000 Lausanne 6
Switzerland
Tel: +41 786 005 109
Email: enquiries@avabooks.ch

Distributed by Thames and Hudson (ex-North America)
181a High Holborn
London WC1V 7QX
United Kingdom
Tel: +44 20 7845 5000
Fax: +44 20 7845 5055
Email: sales@thameshudson.co.uk
www.thamesandhudson.com

Distributed by Sterling Publishing Co., Inc.
in the USA
387 Park Avenue South
New York, NY 10016-8810
Tel: +1 212 532 7160
Fax: +1 212 213 2495
www.sterlingpub.com

in Canada
Sterling Publishing
c/o Canadian Manda Group
One Atlantic Avenue, Suite 105
Toronto, Ontario M6K 3E7

English Language Support Office
AVA Publishing (UK) Ltd.
Tel: +44 1903 204 455
Email: enquiries@avabooks.co.uk

ISBN 2-88479-037-3

10 9 8 7 6 5 4 3 2 1

Design: Bruce Aiken
Picture research: John Dollar
Project management: Nicola Hodgson

Production and separations by
AVA Book Production Pte. Ltd., Singapore
Tel: +65 6334 8173
Fax: +65 6334 0752
Email: production@avabooks.com.sg

a beginner's guide to digital video

peter wells

contents

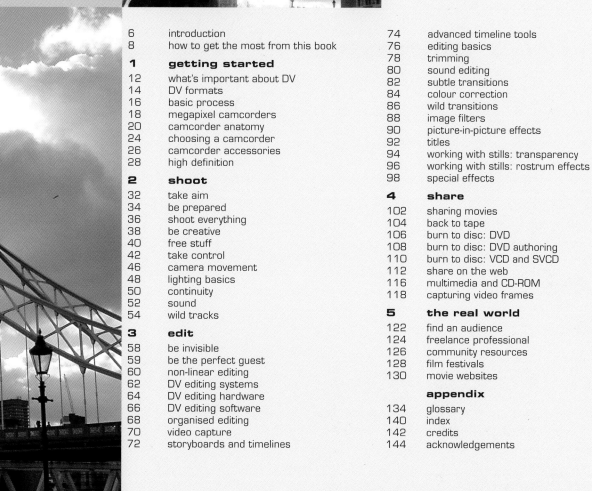

introduction

Mini digital video (MiniDV) was launched as a video format for home users in 1995, but freelance professionals and broadcasters were the first to really take notice, attracted by its quality, portability and price. DV has had a huge impact on the production of wedding videos, corporate presentations and many television shows. Development for the home user has been a slower process, but DV is now ripe for the mainstream. Camcorders are very competitively priced, and video-editing tools are affordable and accessible thanks to the low cost and high performance of today's home computers. Many off-the-shelf Macs and Windows PCs come with video-editing software and DVD recorders installed as standard, and setting up a new machine for video editing has become simple and painless.

DV is a mature market, and it's still growing. Countless new products and technical developments are announced every year. Media tools that were once restricted to the affluent broadcast market are now available on home systems for next to nothing, while the emergence of digital TV and the availability of video streaming on the internet means that there has never been a better time to get your work seen. Regardless of whether you're using video to make a living, make a difference, or just make a record of precious family moments, the processes of storytelling with the moving image are well established and have remained largely unchanged since the early days of cinema. Care, thought, and a good understanding of technique when making a movie cost nothing, but are far more important to a project than the type of camcorder you use or the system you edit with. Knowing how you will achieve your goals will also allow you to make informed decisions on the tools you use – possibly saving a lot of money in the process. Above all else, remember that your audience only cares about what happens on the screen. What you did to get it there and how much it cost is irrelevant.

how to get the most from this book

This book takes a linear, step-by-step approach to movie-making, introducing the fundamental techniques of shooting, editing and publishing one at a time. In each chapter, you'll find guidance on what to look for in hardware and software, as well as examples of how to use it effectively. Above all else, the book is designed to illustrate the workings and potential of desktop video while remaining as agnostic as possible with regard to product itself.

The approach is geared to providing an understanding of media production techniques, and an appreciation of the fact that ideas and creativity make good movies – not the cost of the equipment you use!

introduction
An overview of the theme and techniques set out in the spread.

images
The images are taken from actual digital video projects, providing inspiration as to the breadth and scale of possible subjects.

! *Keep it relevant* Wild effects can be great fun, but they draw a lot of attention to your influence as an editor and often detract from the movie itself. Eccentric alpha wipes and 3D transitions can be right at home in some corporate productions and magazine-type programmes but, even then they can become annoying if overused.

! *Rendering times* Unles using real-time hardwa system, any effect you a project will require rend before it can be played b real-time solutions still effects to be rendered b can be sent out to DV ta FireWire. The longer an complex an effect is, the time it takes to render.

wild transitions

Most video-editing programs provide a vast selection of 'wild' transition effects. You might not need to use any of them, but for many people, the temptation is too great and they go further and buy more in the form of ready-made packs or software kits to help them design their own transition effects. Wild transitions won't necessarily make your video any better (and they could ruin it completely), but if you have to play...

gradient wipes

Gradient wipes (1/2) use black-and-white image files to provide a shape, direction and speed for wipe effects. A gradient wipe would begin in the lightest areas of the image and

progress to the darkes shape of the gradient represents the shape wipe edge; the directio gradient decides the d the wipe; and the rate

1

section title

1/ 2/ A simple gradient wipe transition. Note how the effect follows the gradient path from white to black.

3/ Complex transition editors are available to customise complex 3D transition effects.

4/ Page peels are among the most popular of fancy 3D transitions.

5/ 3D transition effects can be as wild as you like, with particle effects such as this 'shatter' transition.

3 Hollywood FX

editors

Effects fanatics may well find themselves investing in transition editors such as Boris FX or Pinnacle's Hollywood FX [3]. These are plug-in programs that work alongside video-editing software, allowing you to create fancy transitions from scratch. Basic templates can be edited and enhanced, with excellent control over lighting effects on 3D shapes and motion blur. Complex transitions can be keyframed on a timeline, allowing you to decide how long each stage of the effect will take. Transition editors such as this provide excellent levels of control, but they can be expensive and complicated to use. Be absolutely sure that you need these types of effects before you surrender a lot of time and money.

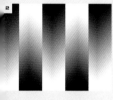

...change within the bitmap image affects its speed. A typical example is a clock wipe, which sweeps round in a circle from the centre of the frame. More creative wipes include smoke and dripping paint effects. Packages such as Pixelan's Spice Rack are available with hundreds of ready-made gradients. You can also create your own gradients for these programs using image-editing tools such as Adobe Photoshop.

3D effects

3D transitions are among the most dynamic and impressive effects available in mainstream editing software. They allow a video clip to take on a three-dimensional form (such as a ball or paper aeroplane) and exit the frame, leaving a new clip in its place. A typical example is the page peel effect, in which one video clip peels away to reveal another behind it [4]. More elaborate variations include shatter effects [5] .in which the outgoing video explodes like shattered glass, and cube spins, in which video clips are displayed on different faces of a rotating cube.

spread title

1 getting started

what's important about DV

Digital video contains a lot of information, resulting in large files and a lot of data transfer during recording or playback. For most purposes, video must be compressed to make it more manageable on normal computers. An extreme example is streaming video for the internet, which has been highly compressed in order to make transfer quick and easy across a modem. Unfortunately this high level of compression causes a reduction in quality.

compression

DV uses a relatively lenient form of compression, which maintains a high level of picture and sound quality, but squashes the data into a package that can be transferred and stored easily on most up-to-date home computers. Compression takes place in the camcorder itself, and the camcorder's digital FireWire connection allows this footage to be copied in its compressed state between digital tapes or between the camcorder and the editing computer. Given the right conditions, these copies, made via FireWire, are lossless – a huge improvement over the old system of video transfer via analogue channels, such as composite video or S-video cables, in which picture and sound quality would degrade with every successive generation.

copying

Lossless copying is a huge bonus for video editors, but you should be aware that data transfers via FireWire don't have the same error correction safeguards that apply when copying files between folders on a computer. Making copies of copies over several generations may cause faults to appear in picture and sound – even if these copies are made digitally. Also, adding special effects to video in an editing system will require that footage to be completely re-processed. How good it looks will depend on the system and software you use.

Nonetheless, DV is the first mainstream video format that allows users to create a finished, edited movie with the same high quality of picture and sound as their original raw footage.

FireWire

Connecting a camcorder to a computer via its digital FireWire interface provides the means for playback to be controlled directly from the computer, rather than locally using its physical buttons. This allows very accurate video capture to the system's hard drive, as well as scene logging and unattended batch capture (more about that later).

FireWire has become a standard part of the modern computer's make-up too. Along with USB, it is slowly replacing SCSI, serial and parallel ports for attaching devices such as scanners, printers and external hard drives. All modern Macs come with built-in FireWire ports, and many Windows-based PCs do too. If they don't, the necessary expansion cards are cheap and

miniDV

easy to install. This standardisation of FireWire connections, and the way in which DV video is accessed through it, means that software developers can now create video-editing programs without worrying about the type of hardware used to import and export footage. This gives you more choice of software, and allows more than one program to be used on the same system if need be (this is a good idea as different editors have different strengths). And, at all levels, DV editing programs provide a rich selection of publishing methods, enabling finished movies to be processed as streaming media for the net; turned into high-quality DVD discs; processed for viewing on handheld computers; or just sent back out to tape.

MiniDV has revolutionised shooting too. Camcorders are small and lightweight – many current models slip easily into a jacket pocket – making it less of a chore to carry one about. The combination of high-quality results and low-end appearance can make it easy to shoot street scenes without attracting the attention of passers-by. Smaller camcorders mean that tripods can be lightweight too, and DV video crews at the professional level find themselves with less heavy grip equipment to lug around.

DV formats

While most people associate the initials 'DV' with the MiniDV camcorder format, there are in fact many different types of digital video. 'Digital video' can mean anything from high-definition footage shot for big-budget movies to a tiny low-bandwidth file crunched for streaming on the net. So be careful when you see products being sold on the strength of 'digital quality' – because that can mean anything!

DV

The most accessible and mature digital video format in the camcorder market is MiniDV. All major camcorder manufacturers make MiniDV models, and the format is easily transferred to home computers via FireWire and supported in all current Windows and Mac operating systems. The 'Mini' prefix isn't there just for show, however. A larger-format DV tape exists, using exactly the same tape format as MiniDV, but contained in a larger cassette housing. These full-size DV tapes can last well over four hours, as opposed to the 60-minute standard (or 83-minute maximum) duration afforded by MiniDV cassettes.

DVCAM

DVCAM is a format reserved for the higher end of the market. It has really only been adopted by its creator, Sony. DVCAM machines record video with the same type of compression as DV (the two are generally indistinguishable to DV editing systems) and the tapes used are the same too. However, DVCAM tapes run at a higher speed than DV, allocating data to a larger area of tape and creating more defined divisions between video and audio tracks on the tape. All this adds up to a more robust recording, less likely to suffer from visual or audible glitches that can occasionally result from faulty tape stock or dirty heads. The trade-off is recording time, however, as a 60-minute DV tape would last only 40 minutes when recorded as DVCAM.

Digital8

Digital8 was introduced in a bid to reduce the cost of digital camcorders by adapting existing analogue technology. Digital8 camcorders record the same type of digital video signal as DV, but recorded to a Hi8 cassette. The bigger tapes mean bigger camcorders, but the prices can be very attractive. Digital8 devices are recognised by video-editing systems as DV models, and behave just as well. Seasoned video enthusiasts moving up to digital video from analogue will also appreciate the ability of Digital8 camcorders to play analogue Hi8 and Video8 tapes, while feeding the signal out via FireWire for capture by a computer in DV format.

MicroMV

MicroMV is the latest tape format to come from Sony. Video is recorded at just under half the data rate of DV, using cassettes 70% smaller than MiniDV tapes. The video format is significantly different to that of DV, DVCAM or Digital8, using a form of MPEG-2 compression – the type of video file used for DVD. At the time of writing, Sony is the only company making MicroMV camcorders, and the format isn't supported by many video-editing programs. Keep an eye on MicroMV, but remember that DV is currently a far more mature format.

2

DVD

The first generation of DVD camcorders recorded only to DVD-RAM discs. These discs are housed in plastic cartridges and, even if the disc is removed, can't be played on the majority of set-top DVD players. DVD-R's appearance in the consumer marketplace has led to the development of DVD camcorders whose recordings are much easier to share. Because of size limitations, these camcorders use small 8cm DVD discs, which accommodate only 30 minutes of good-quality video, and it can be difficult to find shops that stock them. What is more, DVD uses a highly compressed form of MPEG-2 video, which doesn't lend itself well to accurate editing and special effects. DVD is a great format for delivering finished movies, but I wouldn't recommend it as a shooting format if you plan to do anything exciting with your footage later.

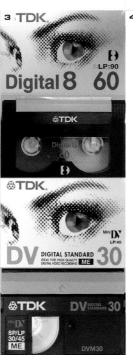

memory cards

Many camcorders now allow you to make video recordings to a memory card. This is a novelty, but it won't deliver anything like the quality of a recording made to DV tape. Memory cards have a relatively small capacity, and can't handle the data transfer rate required for DV, so recordings are made with a high level of compression (typically MPEG-1 or MPEG-4), and a small frame size of up to 320 x 240 pixels. The captured movies are intended to be uploaded to websites and sent in emails – they're not meant to be edited.

basic process

Digital video production can be an administrative nightmare, or a simple, intuitive and organic process, depending on what you want to make and how you choose to make it. The process is always composed of the same three basic stages, however: shooting, editing and sharing.

shooting

Shooting is the practice of gathering footage for a movie. There can be much more to it than simply pointing a camcorder and setting it running. Most professional video shoots are carefully planned out, and the crew go in with a clear idea of what shots are needed and how they will be staged and lit. In drama and in some documentaries, video-makers will shoot a scene or interview several times, allowing them to fine-tune a performance and select just the right take for the final production. Event videographers, on the other hand, have only one opportunity to capture the moment, as you can't re-shoot a wedding or re-run a sports event! They need to be acutely aware of what coverage is required and how best to get it.

Some videos are made using footage that has never really existed. Computer graphics are used in many movies, commercials and TV dramas, and are also becoming the mainstay of video title sequences and links. This footage isn't 'shot' in the traditional sense, but similar decisions regarding composition, pacing and lighting still apply.

editing

Editing is the process in which the raw footage is cut together in sequence. During a shoot, you will be concerned with gathering as much material as possible, but when the editing stage begins, your first priority will be to lose as much of it as you can, to prevent the finished movie from becoming boring. Getting the pacing right for an edit is an art form in itself. Editing involves more than simply laying clips end to end: editors must know how to manipulate picture and sound independently, and be sensible

1

2

3

about when to use special effects, titles and music.

DV footage is captured to the hard drive of a computer, and cut together with dedicated editing software. In most cases, this type of editing is non-destructive – meaning that the actual video files aren't physically split, changed or discarded – allowing editing decisions to be reversed at any time. The one big exception is Apple's iMovie, with which users should be aware that some trimming or editing decisions may be irreversible.

sharing

There are lots of ways to share a finished movie with your audience. The most obvious method is to send it back to tape. This can be done digitally (making an almost perfect clone of the production to DV), or via analogue channels, creating a VHS tape for viewing on a normal VCR. With the right software and hardware, editors can turn their

projects into DVDs too, or crunch them into highly compressed streams for delivery on the internet or inclusion in multimedia presentations. Most good editing tools, regardless of whether they are designed for experts or beginners, provide some degree of support for all these output methods.

megapixel camcorders

1

For anyone with a keen interest in still image photography as well as video, megapixel camcorders may remove the need to carry around more than one camera bag.

megapixel CCDs

The word 'mega', in relation to image resolution, is used to mean 'million'. This means that a megapixel CCD is capable of resolving a million pixels. This is far beyond the needs of ordinary DV video, but the increased resolution comes into its own when capturing digital stills. An image taken from a single-megapixel CCD has a resolution of around 1152 x 864 pixels, and as time goes on, camcorder developers are making models with increasingly higher resolution chips – now surpassing 2Mp – and presenting some serious competition to the digital stills market.

camcorder or camera?

Megapixel camcorders still don't quite touch digital stills cameras for image resolution, and it is taken for granted that as camcorders take leaps in resolution, so too will stills cameras. As an example, when the first 1Mp camcorders were launched, good mainstream stills cameras sported CCDs of around 3Mp. So, while the camcorder could capture an image of 1152 x 864 pixels, the stills camera's maximum image resolution was around 2048 x 1536.

However, it is worthwhile remembering that even a 1Mp image is more than ample for most multimedia presentations,

emails, websites, or anything that presents the picture on a computer screen. Higher resolutions come into their own in print publishing.

The performance gap between digital stills and megapixel video cameras is lessened slightly when shooting on long lenses, however. While camcorders typically feature optical zooms of 10x or more, the zoom of a stills camera rarely exceeds 6x (and is sometimes no more than half that). So, to create a close-up image of a distant object, it may be necessary to crop the picture taken from a digital stills camera, while a camcorder can zoom right in and retain the full available resolution.

memory cards

These high-resolution pictures can't be recorded to DV tape, so megapixel models support memory cards, which behave in much the same way as a floppy disc. There is a range of memory cards out there, and different manufacturers support different types. While SmartMedia and Compact Flash are popular memory formats in digital photography, camcorders are more likely to support MemoryStick or SD Card.

1/ A megapixel camcorder can still be a tiny machine.

2/ A memory card reader is a convenient way to access data from camcorders, cameras, MP3 players and other devices.

3/ 4/ 5/ These images reveal the size comparison between a three-megapixel image from a digital stills camera (3), a one-megapixel image (4) and a DV frame (5).

camcorder anatomy

Camcorder manufacturers update and replace models every season, but they all work in roughly the same way, and are based on the same technology. Knowing how a camcorder works will give you more confidence when buying one, and help you get the most out of it.

CCD

A Charge Coupled Device (CCD) is a small chip that converts light into electrical signals that can be read by the camcorder and recorded to tape. The chip is composed of a matrix of pixels, with each representing a piece of the final image – like a mosaic. Most consumer camcorders have only one CCD, but professional models split incoming light into its primary colours of red, green and blue, processing each individually with an array of 3CCDs [1].

lens

Professional video-makers maintain that the lens is the most important part of a camcorder [2]. Lenses are precision-made, as perfectly cut glass will provide a perfect image. The lenses of domestic DV camcorders are not as finely crafted as those of high-end broadcast cameras, but they're not bad, and some camcorder manufacturers use designer-name lenses for their products to convince you of their high-quality optics.

digital zoom

Many camcorders are sold to the unwary on the strength of their digital zooms [3]. They are often adorned with stickers announcing magnification levels as high as 500x. Don't be fooled! A digital zoom magnifies an image after it has been processed by the CCDs. As you are effectively zooming in to a mosaic of pixels rather than the object itself, picture quality will rapidly deteriorate the closer in you go. There's no avoiding digital zooms on DV camcorders, but they can be turned off, and I'd recommend you do just that!

optical zoom

An optical zoom adjusts elements within the lens to magnify an image before it is processed by the camcorder's CCDs. Magnifying an image before processing allows all available pixels of the CCD to be used, keeping video quality high. Zoom is controlled with a rocker or slider control, placed just under the fingers of the right hand.

microphone

Built-in camcorder microphones can't be relied upon to deliver good sound. For a start, they tend to be multi-directional, meaning that they'll take audio from anywhere. But most importantly, being attached to the camcorder, there is often far too much distance between the mic and the subject – resulting in flat, muddy sound. If you are making a living with video, or are keen to make your movies look and sound great, an external, directional microphone is a must [4/5].

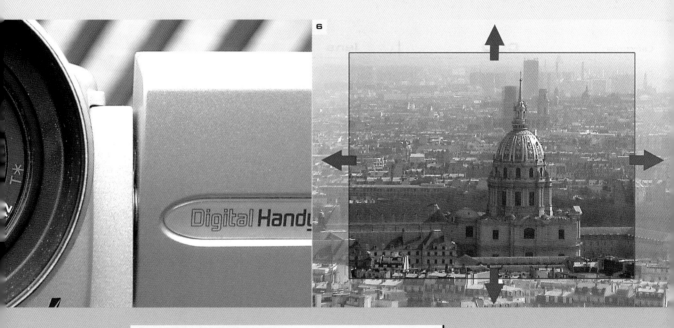

image stabilisers

1/ Camcorders with three CCDs are preferred for professional work.

2/ The lens is the most important part of a camcorder.

3/ Don't be swayed by excessive digital zoom claims!

4/ 5/ Mics can be positioned at the front or the top of a camcorder.

6/ Electronic image stabilisers crop into the picture to help compensate for camera shake.

As with zooms, there are optical image stabilisers, and there are electronic image stabilisers. An optical image stabiliser is a physical device that sits inside the camcorder lens. It responds to sudden and subtle movements of the camcorder, and slightly deflects the incoming light to compensate and reduce the effect of camera shake. As motion compensation happens before the image is processed, the camcorder is able to use the full resolution of its CCDs. Being a physical device, optical image stabilisers are too big to be used in the tiniest pocket camcorders.

Electronic image stabilisers crop into the processed image [6], allocating a central region for the actual recording, with the border acting as a safety zone and used to compensate for camera shake.

Some electronic stabilisers are better than others, but all of them reduce the resolution of the processed image. Quality loss has been lessened in some camcorders with the introduction of high-capacity CCDs, which process far more picture than is needed for the recording, and use the surplus for image stabilisation.

AV sockets

AV sockets provide analogue audio and video output for playback on a TV set or copying to VHS tape [8]. There are two types of analogue video feed available from DV cams: composite video and S-video. Composite video carries all visual information in a single channel, while S-video divides it up into separate colour and tonal feeds. Of the two, S-video provides the better quality. Some camcorders also take in analogue signals via these same sockets for recording to DV tape. It may even be able to channel it straight out of a DV port, allowing old analogue video to be fed straight from analogue tape, through the camcorder to a DV editing system.

7

8

7/ A large LCD monitor can be a great advantage.

8/ Analogue AV sockets and a four-pin FireWire port.

viewfinder

Viewfinders in DV camcorders are small LCD monitors, enclosed in a tube. The nature of the viewfinder is rarely a definitive selling point, but larger viewfinders with high resolutions will be a great help when using the manual settings. The most inexpensive camcorders provide black-and-white viewfinders, while advanced models offer colour. Oddly, very high-end professional camcorders also use black-and-white viewfinders – but these have a much higher resolution and are remarkably clear, making them ideal for monitoring focus and exposure settings.

LCD panel

Flip-out LCD monitors on the sides of camcorders are a feature that developed in the consumer market, and you won't find them on many high-end professional machines [7]. They can be immensely useful, however, and I believe that every camcorder should have one! LCD panels provide a large image, and make it much more comfortable to shoot from very low or high angles, where you wouldn't always be able to see a viewfinder. Be aware that direct sunlight can reflect off LCD panels and make them appear washed-out when shooting outdoors.

AE modes

Among the most useful tools in a DV camcorder's internal programming are AE (auto exposure) modes, providing ready-made settings for handling difficult situations, such as heavily backlit subjects or fast-moving sports events. Other options, such as 'sand' and 'snow', help avoid glare caused by highly reflective environments.

memory cards

Some camcorders carry CCDs with more than a million pixels, enabling capture of high-resolution still images as well as video. These stills are saved to a memory card rather than to tape. There are different types of memory card on the market (most notably MemoryStick, SD Card, MultiMediaCard, SmartMedia and Compact Flash), as numerous companies have devised their own formats and want to make money from the patent. The cards themselves all cost about the same, and work in roughly the same way, however [9]. A camcorder with stills capability will come supplied with a ridiculously small memory card, however, and you will have to buy something bigger.

9

FireWire port

Some companies refer to FireWire as i.Link, and others call it an IEEE1394 interface. Regardless of name, the FireWire port allows DV video to be transferred in its original digital state from tape to tape or between camcorder and video-editing system. It also works as a communication port, allowing playback and recording to be controlled remotely – from the video-editing software, for example. Beware that many camcorders in the EU lack the ability to take in a DV feed via FireWire. This is a move to prevent excessive import duty, but seriously limits the machine's usefulness when editing.

body shape

Small camcorders come in two basic styles: palmcorder or upright [10]. Palmcorders are long machines with a lens at the front and a viewfinder at the back. They sit across your palm and are held like a big metal tube. Upright camcorders are more block-like, with the lens and viewfinder located at the top. The user holds the camcorder by grasping the main body like a pistol grip. Which layout is better depends on the needs of the users, but note that upright models often have a fixed viewfinder that cannot be tilted up, a smaller LCD monitor, and a microphone that points upwards rather than forwards.

9/ Memory cards are invaluable for digital stills.

10/ Two basic body shapes: the palmcorder and upright camcorder.

choosing a camcorder

Camcorders are not cheap, and choosing the right one can be a struggle. The following checklist highlights some of the main points you should look out for when considering a purchase.

CCD

A 3CCD camcorder is preferable for professional work.

Megapixel CCDs provide high-quality stills and better electronic image stabilisation.

image stabilisers

Optical image stabilisers are excellent, but result in a larger camcorder.

Electronic image stabilisers vary in quality, but tend to produce reasonable results alongside high-resolution CCDs.

style and layout

Is an upright or palmcorder design best for you?

Can the viewfinder be tilted up for low-angle shooting?

Is it comfortable to hold?

Do focus and zoom controls fall easily to hand?

Is the camcorder well balanced?

4 **5 6**

lens

Can lens filters and adapters be fitted?

Does the lens have a hood to prevent flare?

How powerful is its optical zoom?

Is manual focus controlled with a ring on the lens barrel? Or an awkward dial tucked out of sight?

connectivity

Is there a microphone socket?

A headphone socket?

A shoe attachment for fitting a directional microphone?

Does it have a working DV input?

Does it have analogue AV inputs?

Will it work as a direct AV-to-FireWire converter?

convenience

Where does the tape load? Some camcorders load from beneath, and that's a huge inconvenience if you use a tripod!

Does it need an additional base station to provide microphone and headphone sockets?

Where are the key manual controls and playback controls? Some camcorders require you to have the monitor open to use them, and that automatically turns the viewfinder off – this is annoying when working in strong daylight.

1/ 2/ 7/ 8/ Some examples of camcorders.

3/ Shoe attachments are useful for mounting extra mics or video lights.

4/ FireWire for video capture and USB for digital stills transfer.

5/ Look out for microphone and headphone sockets.

6/ Check to see how tapes load.

7

8

camcorder accessories

Your camcorder purchase doesn't end with the camcorder. Make sure you have budgeted for the following items.

spare batteries

Extra batteries are a must, and it makes good sense to spend a little extra on long-life batteries if they are available for your make of camcorder.

tripod

Using a tripod can be inconvenient – especially if you're looking forward to the freedom afforded by a tiny camcorder! But taking the time to set up shots on solid legs will greatly improve your video [1]. It also forces you to think more carefully about how the shot is framed.

lens filters

Lens filters [2] can add a stylised tone and texture to your video, but I'd recommend starting off with a simple, clear filter that does nothing to your picture. Attach it to the lens and leave it there. If your camcorder takes any knocks, you'll find it far easier and cheaper to replace a scratched filter than a scratched lens.

3

camera bag

Organise your toolkit with a sensible bag [3/4]. If you're going to be travelling long distances, a hard case might be a better option, but soft, lightweight bags are often sufficient. Don't feel you have to buy a dedicated camera bag, though – look around luggage stores and see if there is anything more discreet that offers the same kind of compartmentalised design. A bag that shouts 'camera inside' can also scream 'steal me'!

4

external mic

For first-rate sound, you ideally want an external microphone that can be held close to the subject [5]. This isn't always possible for one-person shoots, however, but a directional mic mounted on top of the camcorder using its shoe attachment will still be a huge improvement over the built-in microphone.

wide-angle

A common complaint about consumer camcorders is that the wide end of their zooms isn't very wide. A simple adapter screwed onto the front of the camcorder can halve the focal length, giving you a more dramatic wide-angle shot.

lighting accessories

How much lighting gear you need depends greatly on the type of video you want to make, how much money you want to spend, and how much kit you want to carry around with you. A set of small video lights and stands can be an advantage, but always buy them with reflectors, as direct light can look harsh, and be uncomfortable for your on-screen subjects. At the very least, buy a fabric reflector, as this helps fill in shadows when shooting in strong daylight [6].

1/ A tripod is essential for steady shooting.

2/ Filters can affect the image; compensate for difficult conditions; or simply protect the lens.

3/ 4/ Soft camera bags are light, portable and convenient, but flight cases are a safer option for long journeys.

5/ A detachable directional microphone is a very wise investment.

6/ Reflectors are a good idea for reducing contrast in strong daylight conditions.

high definition

MiniDV is having a good run, and seems set to survive for many years yet. But development is now beginning on the next generation of digital camcorders and editing suites, and the buzzword seems to be 'high definition'.

high-definition TV

High-definition TV (HDTV) has a much higher pixel resolution to standard video formats (such as MiniDV and DVD) or current TV broadcast. Done well, high-definition video can look as good as cinema, and producers of TV drama have already started to move away from film and shoot on high-definition video instead. However, almost all this work is still being broadcast at standard definition resolutions, and it might be a long while yet before TV stations begin broadcasting high-definition signals.

First of all, broadcast equipment is expensive, and production companies are normally reluctant to replace it unless it is broken beyond repair or obsolete. So adopting an entirely new broadcast standard overnight is an economic nightmare. Secondly, the recent developments in digital broadcasting have been focused on squeezing as many channels into an allotted bandwidth as possible – and that means high levels of compression, and a drop in picture and sound quality. Changing the agenda of lowering broadcast quality to one of greatly improving it will take a completely new mindset in the broadcast industry. And finally, the introduction of HDTV will require viewers to change their TV sets for high-definition models at a time when many of us have just taken the step to 16:9 widescreen sets.

why bother?

Even if broadcasters are reluctant to move to high definition, and DVD retains its place as the most popular home video standard, high-definition video still makes a lot of sense for professional work. As with any form of recording media, it is important to start with the very best format for acquisition. A high-definition recording will look stunning when compressed for standard-definition delivery on TV or DVD.

What's more, digital video has long been adopted by maverick film-makers, who shoot on tape, and have the final cut printed to film for theatrical release. The Dogme movement of film-makers made good use of DV for its immediacy and simplicity, for example. High definition offers the same level of convenience, but delivers a much richer image for film transfer.

first consumer models

The first consumer-level high-definition camcorders were launched by JVC in 2003. The models record a widescreen image with dimensions of 1280 x 720, as opposed to DV video, which weighs in at 720 x 576 pixels (PAL) or 720 x 480 (NTSC – see page 105). The GR-HD1 is the first in what's sure to become a long line of high-definition camcorders, and JVC has made a smart move in recording its HD signal to MiniDV cassettes. Not only does this ensure that media is affordable and easy to find, but it allows the camcorder to double as a standard MiniDV model too. Perhaps the biggest initial concern about the new generation of affordable HD camcorders comes from the fact that they use a form of MPEG-2 video compression, which isn't ideal for frame-accurate editing.

support

As the first high-definition camcorders are launched, there's no support for the new video format in any mainstream DV editing application. This is to be expected, however, as new formats and standards are never adopted or supported by everyone overnight. Lossless capture and output of the HD video signal should be easy to implement, as the camcorders still use a FireWire interface, but frame-accurate editing might be more tricky, due to the MPEG compression methods used.

1/ High-definition camcorders have finally reached the consumer market.

2 shoot

take aim

Your entire movie relies on the shoot. Don't be fooled by the sophistication of video-editing software and special effects tools. If your video footage is poor, there's very little you can do to save it. Taking time to make your video look and sound good from the start will pay off greatly when you come to edit. Good footage lends itself to freedom and creativity in the cutting room, allowing you to tell your story rather than waste time plastering over cracks.

Good lighting and appropriate use of a tripod helps, but the main ingredient in any shoot should be thought. Good planning, strong ideas, and careful execution cost nothing and yield excellent results.

Knowing what you want and how you'll get it with the available time, resources and money is half the work of making a movie. And once the camera's rolling, nothing should dissuade you from getting the shots you want. Never be put off going for that killer shot just because it looks like 'too much hassle' on the day. That killer shot will go a long way to making an outstanding movie!

1/ A sample script marked up with tramlines indicating what type of shots are to be used in the scene.

2/ Scenes from a storyboard created in Curious Labs' Poser.

3/ Curious Labs' Poser can be a great help with storyboarding if drawing isn't one of your strengths. Finished scenes can be exported as high-quality colour images; sketch-style pictures such as those used here; or even animated and rendered as video clips. Detailed 3D backgrounds can also be made in programs such as Corel's Bryce.

4/ Take time to scout locations. Get a feel for the layout of the area and take photos for reference if necessary.

2

be prepared

Many camcorder users are happy to go through a simple process of point-and-shoot with no desire to turn their footage into a polished movie. For the rest of us, planning and preparation is often a key part of the movie-making process. Dramas, corporate videos, instructional movies, and even documentaries benefit from being thoroughly planned on paper.

script

Scripts can be as detailed or as simple as you like. For dramas, corporate videos, historical documentaries, and all other tightly controlled projects, scripts are written to provide all dialogue and key action. Scripts are divided into scenes, to help keep track of setting, time and context, but seldom contain any specific shooting or editing information.

The film and TV industries work to standard screenplay formats, designed to clearly separate dialogue and action. Script writers are encouraged to leave as much white space on the page as possible by not packing the text too tightly. This makes it easier for actors, technicians and investors to read, but also provides ample space for annotation as the shoot draws nearer. Examples of screenplays from established movies can be found on the internet or in any good bookshop.

'Tramlining' [1] is a simple method of deciding how the script will be covered by the cameras. Lines are drawn down the page to denote where particular types of shot will be used. To allow more flexibility at the editing stage, it is common practice to overlap shots, or to shoot key scenes two or three times in different ways.

1

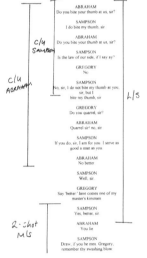

Even open documentaries and event videos can benefit from a loose form of script. You can't tell people how to behave or what to say, but you should still have a fair idea of the people and events that need to be covered throughout the course of the shoot.

storyboards

Storyboards provide a visual reference to the planned shots [2]. They help provide an early idea of how the movie will look, and avoid possible continuity errors (was the main character looking to the right of the frame or to the left?). Storyboards are for reference only and don't need to be works of art, but the more detail they contain the better. Drawing storyboards is a

locations

Know where you're going to be working. If it is outdoors, do you have a contingency plan if it starts to rain? Have you checked the weather forecast? Is mains power required for the shoot? And if so, where are the most convenient power points?

Know how the available light falls at the times of day that you plan to shoot, and keep an eye out for good opportunities, such as interesting vantage points for creative shots or foreground details that can help frame an image in a more interesting way [4]. If the shoot is a wedding or similar event, try to picture the location full of people, and plan your routes from place to place so you can be everywhere you need to be well ahead of time.

Paris - Pompidou 1

Paris - Pompidou 2

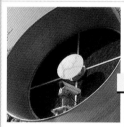

Paris - Pompidou 3

crew

Can the shoot be done single-handed? The more equipment you use, the more help you will need. Even simple tasks such as holding reflectors and microphones in place can require a second pair of hands. Having assistance saves a lot of time and stress. Friends and family can make invaluable crew members, so don't be afraid to ask for help.

schedule

Plan your time carefully. Shoots such as weddings won't allow you much control over the timetable of events, but dramas and documentaries should work around you. Keep it realistic – don't think that you can shoot a three-hour epic in one day just because you can do it on paper.

Consider how much light is available for exterior shots. Also work out how much time each shot will take to set up, moving cameras and positioning lights, reflectors and microphones. On the day of the shoot, it always feels better to be ahead of schedule than behind!

checklist

Items such as the camcorder, tripod, microphone and lights are easy to remember, but you may also need things like duct tape to secure trailing cables (safety is important!). Are there any set pieces or props that you need to bring with you? Have you brought enough cash to cover unexpected parking expenses? And finally, if you're enlisting people to work as crew members or cast, you must remember to feed them!

---

very worthwhile practice, giving an immediate visual reference to the work in hand, helping to eliminate a lot of last-minute decision-making and forcing you to think through the movie thoroughly before shooting.

If drawing or painting truly isn't your forte, however, there are 3D graphics programs available that can be used for storyboarding. Curious Labs'

Poser was used to create the storyboards pictured here [2] and [3]. This sophisticated software allows three-dimensional human and animal figures to be created, clothed and posed. Users have just as much control over the (virtual) camera and lighting as the characters themselves.

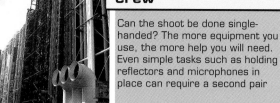

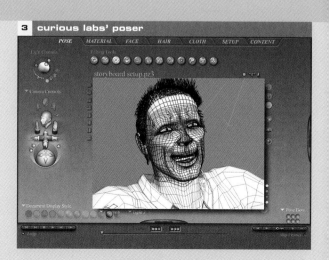

3 curious labs' poser

Establishing shots Masters are, typically, wide shots in which all action is shown or suggested. They provide a sense of orientation for the viewer, showing clearly how the subjects are positioned in relation to one another. In this example [1], we see establishing shots of a band playing in a crowded nightclub. All band members are visible, but these wide master shots can be taken from different angles in order to place different band members in the foreground or even to face directly into the audience.

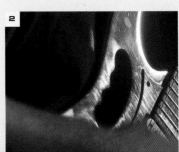

shoot everything

No matter how meticulously a shoot has been planned, it's rarely safe to assume that you've got enough footage. The moment editing starts, you'll discover new ways to express ideas or represent the events at hand. You may also spot mistakes that went unnoticed at the time and need patching over. Taking the time to cover new angles and shoot extra details will provide the freedom to be daring at the editing stage, and to hide any unwanted hiccups. But above all else, it's important to be able to take a step back from the plan that you've committed to paper, and be open to any new elements that could make your final movie shine.

Close-ups These bring the audience right in to the action. In an instructional video, close-ups are used to demonstrate how a specific task is accomplished. In drama, they're used to evoke a more emotional response. In our example [2], close-ups are used to give emphasis to the roles of individual band members with strong close-ups of the singer's face or details of guitars and drums.

Medium shots A typical medium shot is of a person framed from the waist up. In essence, it is a step in from the wide establishing shot, and helps emphasise the role played by an individual within a scene. Medium shots don't

Reactions Action is only a small part of drama. How those actions affect others can often be more important. Reaction shots help provide a tone and context for a scene and also help influence the audience's own emotional responses. In an interview situation, reaction shots typically take the form of nods and other appropriate reactions from the interviewer – and many of these are shot after the interview has finished! In an action movie, you'll often see the terrified faces of bystanders in more explosive scenes. In this example [4], we're following the reactions of the audience, to show how they are often as important a part of the show as the band itself.

1/ Establishing the scene.
2/ Close-ups.
3/ Medium shots.
4/ Reactions.
5/ Cutaways.

Cutaways Cutaway shots are close-up details of anything and everything relevant to a scene. For an interview video, you may choose to cut away to the interviewee's hands gesticulating. If the interview concerns a physical object, such as a book, you might want a cutaway shot of the book itself. In drama, movie-makers often spend whole days shooting cutaways of all handheld props used within a scene, such as cigarettes being lit or keys being turned in locks, as any one of them could come in useful during the editing process. In the case of our concert footage,

we've pulled aside some audience shots in which people aren't clearly singing along with the band [5]. These can be used anywhere in the movie, and if our camerawork becomes weak at any point, we can use them to cover up mistakes.

need to be restricted to one person, however. In this example [3], we're able to frame one person in a medium shot while another is shown in the background in a long shot.

be creative

Careful framing and the creative use of your camcorder and environment contribute greatly to the look of a movie and cost nothing. Don't just place the camcorder at a random position and start shooting – think about foreground, background, lighting and composition.

dividing your frame

The video frame is a rectangle with an aspect ratio of 4:3 (or 16:9 if you are shooting for a widescreen TV). How people and objects are arranged within that frame goes a long way towards making a visually exciting movie. Good framing and exciting composition are largely a matter of subdividing the video frame into smaller shapes of different sizes and proportions.

Take any rectangle, and draw a line through it, dividing it into two boxes. Try dividing the boxes further. You will often find that uneven divisions are far more interesting than even ones. When it comes to framing a video shot, think about how on-screen elements such as horizons, doors, walls, people and props bisect the frame. Use them to divide it in a way that looks interesting to you. Try using these lines of division to lead the viewer's eye, emphasising on-screen elements without having to resort to big close-ups [1].

Foreground framing B-movie Westerns would often use props such as wagon wheels in the foreground of a shot to subdivide it in interesting ways. The technique applies equally well to windowpanes, doorways and any other structural device that can provide a frame within a frame [2]. Don't be afraid to put objects between the camera and subject.

Make your on-screen characters a part of their surroundings.

Background framing Background objects can be used as frames too, giving emphasis to foreground elements. For example, framing a person against a large square building can give them a sense of separation from the rest of the frame, emphasising their presence and importance more than if they were set against a random background. Look at your surroundings for features that can help isolate key characters where appropriate.

dramatic angles

It can be tempting to shoot everything from your own eye level, but that can make for confrontational (or just plain boring) footage. High and low vantage points add a little more interest to a frame. Think carefully about whose world you are trying to convey. For example, a children's birthday party should be shot from a child's eye-level to present the world from their perspective. What's more, don't feel the need to meet every person face-on. A slight angle or a profile is often more comfortable than direct eye-to-eye confrontation.

reflections

If your setting features water, glass, or mirrored surfaces, shooting reflections can give lovely results – particularly if the reflective surface is curved or textured. It's not usually a good idea to shoot a lot of video this way, but effects such as this can provide an interesting way to begin scenes – or provide good cutaway shots.

perspective

As well as dividing your frame in two dimensions, take care over the way in which objects relate to each other in space. Careful use of a camcorder's zoom lens can give immense control over perspective, making settings seem vast and roomy [3] or compact and claustrophobic [4]. Wide-angle lens adapters are a great tool for adding depth to a shot, while zooming in close can make busy crowds seem unbearably dense.

extreme close-ups

In movies, extreme close-ups are often used to pick out an actor's or a subject's eyes [5]. They can evoke an intense feeling of urgency, or help inform the audience of a player's emotional state. Extreme close-ups can also be used as illustrative graphic devices – following mercury up a thermometer to indicate climbing temperatures, for example. These details help involve the audience in the movie. They shouldn't be overused, but it is useful to shoot them and have them available at the editing stage – you never know when something will need explaining.

1/ This image shows how objects in a frame can be arranged to lead the viewer's eye into the scene.

2/ Think about framing your subject in an unusual way – here, the circular shape of a tunnel in a children's playground makes for an eye-catching device.

3/ 4/ These two frames show how excessive focal lengths can exaggerate or crush perspective.

5/ Extreme close-ups have good visual impact and can help add drama to a scene.

1/ The harsh desert sunlight is exploited to highlight the arresting shape of the camel caravan against the horizon.

2/ Artificial lighting in this shot creates a striking silhouette as well as bringing out the texture of the background.

3/ Colourful Buddha statues create an atmospheric backdrop to a shoot in Nepal. You don't need to travel to such exotic places to find interesting settings, however – exploit your surroundings.

4/ Foreground motion can be just as effective as camera movements. This scene uses a children's fairground ride to sweep past the frame. The image appears active, while the camera and subject remain static.

free stuff

As a movie-maker, your responsibility is to put all available money on the screen. Taking advantage of free resources will allow more of your budget to be allocated to other areas and increase the movie's production values.

the sun

Sunlight can provide ample illumination for a movie, but it has its limitations. For a start, shooting time is limited, so you need to plan working days carefully to get the most from the available light. Also, the direction of sunlight changes during the day, as the Earth turns. Aim to get all wide establishing shots done in one short session before moving in for close-ups. This allows the position of actors to be changed in close-up to compensate for lighting changes without interfering with the overall look of a scene. Also, a change in the amount of cloud cover can affect the nature of light from the sun. A clear sky will provide very hard lighting and strong solid shadows [1], while clouds act as diffusers, creating a subtle light and shadows with soft edges.

artificial light

Night-time shooting can be greatly enhanced by taking advantage of the garish lighting available in city centres, particularly flashing neon signs and decorative glitterball effects. If this is your only source of illumination, you are probably better off shooting as many close-ups as possible, as shadow detail in the backgrounds of wide shots will be minimal, but don't be afraid to present your subject as a silhouette to create more drama [2]. Slowing shutter speeds for night-time shots will produce trailing effects, which can look

locations

It should be easy to find impressive settings for your shoots. Almost every town or city is within easy reach of effective landscapes, cityscapes or architecture to provide a backdrop for a movie. Use them well. Think about how a background can frame your subjects, and work to create whatever sense of depth or confinement is appropriate to the scene. A good setting can provide context and credibility to movies, so don't take it for granted [3].

3

4

motion

The human eye is instinctively drawn to motion. Simple camera movement can help hold the viewer's interest, and you may be able to use your surroundings to provide a free ride without the need for bulky or expensive tracks or jibs. Think about using escalators, exterior glass elevators, or even funfair rides to give your camera life [4]. Foreground action can be impressive too. Try shooting through a spinning carousel or across a busy road, allowing fast-moving objects to sweep past in the foreground. Objects momentarily obscuring the frame as they pass by can provide effective cutting points when you come to edit the movie. Keep focus on manual, however, to stop it automatically shifting between the foreground and background.

quite effective around brightly coloured neon lights. You can also try experimenting with streetlights and car headlights (just remember to keep off the road).

aperture

The aperture is an iris, which regulates how much light comes into the lens. Opening the iris allows more light in, aiding exposure in dimly lit conditions. The aim when controlling exposure is to get just the right level of detail in shadows and highlights. Automatic exposure works on the assumption that the overall tone for a frame will average out as a mid-grey, but this isn't always the case in the real world. You will also find that automatic settings cause very noticeable and ugly changes when panning past bright elements such as lamps or windows.

take control

Automatic controls on consumer camcorders can be reasonably good, but relying on them too much cuts you off from a lot of creative possibilities. The only way to produce movies with the look and feel that you want is to be brave and control the camcorder manually.

focus

Automatic focus controls can have a habit of 'hunting' – that is, moving in and out, trying to decide which part of the frame should be sharp. Hunting can be especially bad in low light conditions. Taking manual control means that you decide what is important in the frame, and ensures that focus won't be thrown off by passing objects in the foreground [1].

To focus manually, zoom in closely on your subject, adjust focus until the image is sharp, then zoom back out. Zoom won't affect focus at all, but it will provide big details to use as reference. If the subject is a person, make your point of focus the eyes – that is where the viewers will be looking [2].

1/ Manual focus was necessary to catch this shot – automatic controls would have settled on the fine criss-crossing bars. Focusing on the owl has thrown the bars so far out of focus that they're almost invisible.

2/ A combination of close zoom and wide iris contributes to a narrow depth of field – useful for separating foreground from background.

shutter speed

Shutter speed determines how long each frame is exposed to light. Slow shutter speeds let in more light and must be accompanied by a smaller aperture setting to attain correct exposure. They also give rise to exaggerated motion blur. For that reason, sports events and fast-moving objects are often shot with extremely high shutter speeds, keeping the image as sharp as possible [3]. This requires a wider aperture to let in more light, and that in turn restricts your depth of field.

white balance

Light sources that we perceive to be white seldom are actually white. Colour temperature is a term used to describe different types of light source and the actual colours that they emit. Our brains instinctively adjust their perception of these colours to make them appear white, but camcorders often need to be told what kind of light you're using. At some levels of production, there's a need to carefully measure colour temperature, but for most applications, it's sufficient to understand that sunlight appears blue on camera, while tungsten light appears orange. Setting a camcorder's white balance provides a point of reference for the machine, allowing it to reproduce colours the way you see them rather than the way they actually appear. All DV camcorders provide indoor and outdoor white balance options to compensate for the different colour temperatures of tungsten and sunlight. Some also allow white balance to be set manually, using actual white objects for reference. This is useful if you are working with mixed light sources or fluorescent lights.

3

4

focus pull

Working with a small depth of field allows you to divert the audience's attention without moving the camera or cutting to a new shot. Simply shifting focus from foreground to background can have a dramatic impact on the shot [4], and this technique is used all the time in mainstream movies. It also allows objects moving towards the camera to be kept sharp at all times.

Focus pulling is a tricky business. Big-budget productions hire dedicated technicians to act solely as focus pullers, and they rely on having cameras with fully calibrated focus controls that can be accurately set according to distance. Consumer camcorders don't provide that level of quantitative control – and their focus rings keep turning and turning forever, so you can't even mark them up yourself. The technique is possible, but it requires patience, practice, and a good eye – don't expect to get it right on the first take!

3/ A shutter speed of 1/10,000 second was used to 'freeze' the droplets of water in the first image. Definition is completely lost in the second image, which was shot with a much slower shutter speed.

4/ Focus pulls are a very effective method of directing the viewer's attention.

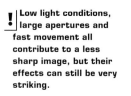 **Low light conditions, large apertures and fast movement all contribute to a less sharp image, but their effects can still be very striking.**

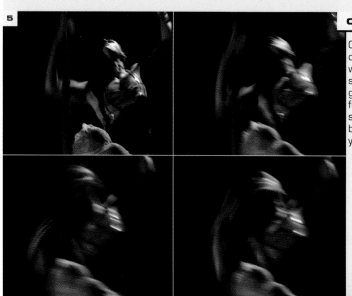

5

Once you have mastered your camcorder's manual controls, you will be in a position to create some striking visual effects to greatly enhance your movie. The following are commonly used stylistic techniques, and cannot be created with any confidence if you are using automatic controls!

depth of field

Depth of field is the range of distance from the camera lens in which objects are in focus. It is determined by two factors: aperture and focal length. Depth of field increases with a smaller aperture and a wide-angle lens, and decreases when you zoom in or open up the iris. While a small depth of field requires more work in focusing and framing, it can also yield a more interesting and film-like composition. Keeping a scene's background soft helps the subject stand out. It also makes the overall frame more dynamic and helps steer the attention of viewers to areas that you feel are important.

Opening the iris fully to reduce depth of field can be tricky in sunlit environments, however, as you risk overexposing the image. A faster shutter speed might help, but this will also reduce motion blur and could give rise to a slight strobing effect if there is a lot of motion in the shot. Some camcorders have neutral density (ND) filters built-in. Applying an ND filter reduces the amount of light coming in through the lens and allows the iris to be opened a little wider still. If the camcorder's ND filter doesn't cut out enough light – or if it doesn't have one at all – add-on filters can be bought very cheaply from camera stores, and will screw onto the front of the lens. Make sure you know the camcorder's filter diameter when asking for one.

7

silhouette or halo?

Some high-contrast situations provide a number of creative options that won't be explored by a camcorder's automatic controls. For example, if a background is more brightly lit than the subject, you have a choice of exposing for the background (dropping the subject into shadow) or setting exposure correctly for the subject, in which case the background will be heavily overexposed and could result in a halo effect. Both approaches will give dramatic results, but evoke a very different feel.

5/ A deliberately slow shutter speed was used to create this enhanced sense of motion blur.

6/ 7/ Backlit scenes will force you to choose between an underexposed foreground (6) or an overexposed background (7). Both can have a high dramatic impact.

off-white balance

Setting the white balance using actual white objects for reference can produce accurate colour reproduction, but careful use of off-white objects can make the overall image warmer or cooler, enhancing the feel of the movie. Some accuracy and control of this technique can be had in using Warm Cards. These are used as the white reference object, and are specifically designed to provide stylistic control over a shot's colour balance, warming or cooling it as required.

camera movement

For many projects, it's wise to provide support for your camcorder rather than shooting handheld. This doesn't mean that footage has to be static, however. A well thought-out camera movement can be invaluable in setting a scene or evoking a sense of fluidity and motion. Some camera moves are easily achieved on a tripod, but some require specialised supports. But, as with all aspects of movie production, there are always affordable alternatives – or ways to cheat!

pan and tilt

Pans and tilts are by far the most common camera movements, and can be performed on most basic tripods. A tilt, as its name suggests, is achieved by tilting the tripod head up or down – be it to follow a linear motion such as an elevator; scan the surface of a building [1]; or follow the direction of a long, straight road. A pan is created by turning the tripod head from side to side. Use it to keep the camera trained on a person or object that's passing by, or to dwell on broad landscapes that can't be fully captured in a static frame [2].

Be aware that any jerkiness will stand out when panning or tilting, so be careful – a good fluid head tripod will help matters greatly. Also, try to ease each movement in and out rather than allowing it to suddenly start and stop. The speed of pans and tilts will greatly influence the tone of the video you're shooting. A slow pan can appear leisurely and relaxing, while quick 'whip' pans add great urgency to a scene. However you want to do things, keep them interesting. If your move is a slow one, try to ensure that there's something in frame that can hold the audience's attention – and if it's leading the movement, so much the better!

track

As its name suggests, 'tracking' involves the movement of a camcorder along a track, providing a smooth, linear motion. The move typically uses a 'dolly', which may take the form of a platform on which the tripod is placed, or it may be a large contraption supporting the camera and providing a seat for the operator. Inexpensive and smaller-scale options for lightweight cameras include lightweight dollies designed to run on aluminium ladders.

Tracking forwards or backwards makes a great alternative to zooming. While zooming has no effect on the relative placement of objects in a frame, tracking forwards and back takes full advantage of perspective within a scene, with closer objects moving more quickly than distant ones. It also allows the viewer to feel as if they are part of the action, moving into or out of the frame.

Tracking left or right with a moving person or object brings the viewer into a scene without the voyeuristic sense that accompanies forward-moving point-of-view shots. This also enables the camera to remain with the action much more effectively than a simple pan on a static tripod. Tracks can also be given bends, thereby allowing movement around objects.

1/ 2/ Pans and tilts are simple to perform by swinging the camcorder round on a tripod from side to side or up and down.

jibs and cranes

Jibs and cranes do almost the same job, but to different degrees. A crane can lift a camcorder to great heights, providing impressive shots down on your subject or rising up to meet the action face to face should there be something fascinating happening on your chimney. Cranes are not always costly – there are some good lightweight versions that balance well with DV camcorders and work as attachments to standard tripods – but the sheer height of them means that an additional LCD monitor is required if you are going to see what you are shooting. The monitors can often cost more than the crane itself.

A jib serves much the same purpose as a crane, but has a smaller reach. A jib might only extend to a height of three metres, but that can still deliver a very dramatic high shot for many scenes. The arm's compactness means that it can be used for normal shooting too, offering a lot more versatility than a basic static tripod.

Jibs also give the ability to bring the camera low as well as high. Tipping the arm the other way makes it possible to shoot from very low angles without having to compromise on control or comfort.

camera stabilisers

Big-budget features use Steadicam rigs to provide fluid motion when tracks and jibs are too impractical. The hardware is hugely expensive and requires great skill to operate, but the theory behind Steadicam has been applied to some small and affordable stabilisers for lightweight DV camcorders.

They work by balancing the camcorder on a small spindle and using a counterweight to provide balance. They can be quite heavy, and don't provide the same solidity of controlled motion that you get from tracks and jibs, but they are useful tools if you need to work handheld but don't want a typically 'handheld' look.

1

! *Move for a static shot* One of the most effective uses for camera movement is to keep the subject static in frame. For example, all televised athletics events have long camera tracks running alongside the running tracks for sprints and relays; the camera is kept moving with the runners, ensuring that the leader is kept in the same position of the frame at all times.

2

! *Moving lights* Moving lights can be used to create a sense of motion within a scene. For example, actors in a static car can be made to look as if they are driving if they are occasionally swept with small spots to simulate the headlights of oncoming vehicles.

! *Coloured light* Adding coloured gels to lights can provide strong dramatic effects – but be careful not to over-saturate your scene and completely lose its indigenous colour!

lighting basics

Good use of light can have a massive effect on your video. Light can be used to pick out important subjects, and lose unwanted detail. It can also be used to create drama and enhance the mood of a scene. You don't need access to an expensive studio to use light effectively either – a little lateral thinking and a basic understanding of how light works can help you create some great results.

key light

A key light is the main source of illumination for a shot. For an outdoor shoot, this light will probably be the sun. If an artificial key light is needed, think carefully about where to place it. Lighting a scene from the same position as the camcorder will result in a flat image with little depth or texture, while lighting from the sides introduces more shadow and contrast. Using a very directional key light directly from above will plunge eye sockets into shadow and create a rather oppressive feel. Lighting a person from below produces unnatural results, often associated with clichéd horror movies.

fill light

A strong key light will create shadows. If the tonal difference between shadows and highlights is too great, you will be left with a very high-contrast image. This is fine for some dramatic contexts, but a more natural feel can be achieved by filling in the shadows to bring out more detail. Additional lights will do the job, but you can also get the effect you need by bouncing light back into shadow areas using a reflective surface, such as a Lastolite reflector or a sheet of polystyrene.

backlighting

Backlighting typically serves to provide slight highlighting around the edges of subjects, helping them to stand out from the background. Backlighting is particularly effective in giving definition to shoulders and hair, and can be extremely useful when shooting against a blue screen for compositing and special effects.

1/ This shot makes use of a key light and fill for the subject's face, but keeps backlighting to a minimum, allowing her to fall into shadow.

2/ A single, hard key light is used here to create a high-contrast image with very little shadow detail.

! *Flags and barn doors* Dedicated video lights come with hinged barn doors, which can be used to direct the way light falls, allowing more control over what gets lit and what is left in shadow. Professional movie-makers often take even more control with black flags – fireproofed fabric stretched over a metal frame. Flags are set up on stands, and are positioned to keep certain areas of the scene in shadow.

! *Fireproofing* Tungsten lights get very hot. If you are using fabric flags and diffusers in your lighting set-up (or putting anything in close proximity to the bulbs), make sure that they are thoroughly fireproofed. Never set up strong lighting next to curtains or other hanging fabrics.

hard and soft light

Light can be hard or soft. Hard light is very directional and creates strong shadows with solid edges. It can be created by small pinpoint light sources, or very distant sources – if the sky is clear, sunlight is one of the hardest sources of light available to you (see page 40). Soft light creates subtle shadows with soft edges, and is caused by large light sources, whose rays are emitted in many different directions. Direct sunlight is a difficult source to soften. Cloud cover does the job nicely, but you are hardly in control of the weather. For indoor shoots, the easiest way to soften a tungsten light is to bounce it off the ceiling. Alternatively, there are gauzes and translucent fabrics available that can act as diffusers and spread light over larger areas.

textured light

Just as placing objects in front of the camera can divide up a frame and give a more interesting composition, the same approach can be taken with objects placed in front of the key light. Try placing wooden slats or warped bubble glass between the light and the subject, and see how the resulting shadows can be used to separate elements of the composition. Also, try bouncing light off reflective surfaces, such as water to add texture to a scene (but be sure to keep any liquids away from electrics).

! *Balance your colours* Remember that sunlight and tungsten have very different colours (see page 42). If you are mixing the two, add a blue gel to the tungsten lights so that the colours match.

3 4

3/ Here, a key light and fill are used, along with a backlight to pick out shoulders and hair, creating a strong definition between subject and background.

4/ With a clear sky, sunlight is the hardest light source available. Note the high contrast and well-defined shadows in this shot.

continuity

It is easy to overlook fine details during a shoot, but careless mistakes and inconsistencies can ultimately spoil the seamless flow of an edited production. Did someone pick up a glass with their right hand or their left? Did they stand to leave at the same point in the script for each shot? Was that wine stain always there? How on-screen talent handles dialogue and props is essential to good continuity within a scene – but your own technical and creative

180-degree line

Cutting between shots can leave the viewer disorientated unless some basic rules are adhered to. During an action shot, think about the direction your subject is moving in the frame. A sprinter moving from the left of the frame to the right in a long shot should still be moving left to right when you cut to a close-up. A change of direction relative to the frame will give the impression that the runner has changed direction. Try to imagine a line indicating the path of your subject's motion. So long as you stay on one side of the line, you can place the camera anywhere without affecting the continuity of movement between shots [1]. If the line is crossed, the subject will appear to have switched directions!

Take the same approach when shooting dialogues. Imagine a similar line stretching between people in an interview situation or a dramatic confrontation. Keeping the camera on one side of that line for wide shots, close-ups and cutaways will maintain the sense that your subjects are facing each other. If you step over the line at any time, one of your characters will appear to have suddenly turned away.

decisions are equally as important to producing a seamless video sequence.

1/ In this sequence, the line of movement for the rollerbladers is clearly marked by a line of plastic cups. Crossing that line between shots would disorientate the viewer.

2/ 3/ A similar line can be imagined – such as the eye line between this street performer and his audience.

eye lines

Viewers are instinctively drawn to the eyes of any people depicted in video, and they are always well aware of where people are looking (2/3). An actor whose gaze is wandering is easy to spot, so it is important that they have something or someone to focus on at all times. On which side of the camera their eye line falls is important too. Looking straight into the camera lens is often too confrontational for the audience, but allowing the eye line to fall on the wrong side of the camera can be disorientating. Use the rule of the 180-degree line with people's eye lines, just as you would with more obvious action.

quiet on set!

Listen carefully to your surroundings before you start shooting. Background noises caused by fluorescent lighting, fridges and the like will probably go unnoticed by you, but they will be very obvious on the finished recording. If you are shooting in locations such as bars or clubs, make sure that the jukebox is unplugged and the DJ is on a break, as background music will badly affect audio continuity at the editing stage (the record will 'jump' at every cut). Noise that is accidentally recorded during a shoot is very difficult to remove from the soundtrack – and unwanted music is virtually impossible to get rid of!

2

3

lighting continuity

Drawing a quick sketch of an interior lighting set-up before shooting will be a big help if you need to come back and re-shoot footage at a later stage. A change in lighting from one shot to the next can be very noticeable. When shooting outdoors, remember that the direction of sunlight changes throughout the course of the day, so try to move with it. Shoot all your wide shots in the morning, then move in for your close-ups afterwards, changing the position of actors if necessary to keep light coming in from the same direction, and maintaining the relative position of shadows and highlights. Keep an eye on the sky too, as increased cloud cover will soften light and change the tone of your footage from one shot to the next.

! Headphones When working with microphones, always monitor your sound with a good pair of headphones. Plugging a microphone into your camcorder will disable the on-board mic, so it is essential that you listen in to ensure the new microphone works and you're not just shooting mute footage. If possible, go for big DJ-style headphones, which cut out surrounding noises, allowing you to concentrate on the recorded audio.

sound

A great soundtrack can make good video dazzling, while dull sound can dampen even the most breathtaking visuals. Audio has an enormous effect on setting a tone for your movie, and also tells the audience what is happening outside of the visual frame.

microphones

1

Don't rely on your camcorder's built-in microphone to provide good sound; chances are that it won't. People are good at cutting through the natural cacophony of everyday surroundings to isolate specific voices or sounds. Machines are not so clever – they will record whatever the microphone feeds them. If you are not careful, you will be left with a big mush of audio that is almost impossible to work with.

Invest in a directional microphone. The built-in mics on camcorders are multi-directional, meaning that they pick up sound from all around. A directional microphone will only pick up sounds clearly if you point it at them, allowing you to isolate individual sounds in relatively noisy environments. There are many such mics designed for video-makers, and they can be mounted on the camcorder's shoe attachment (if it has one). This is useful if you are working on your own and don't have anyone on hand to help with sound. Some of these models have a zoom option, enabling you to decide just how directional you want them to be.

Other types of microphone to consider are tie-clip mics and handheld reporters' microphones. Tie-clip mics attach to the subject's clothing, and are designed only to pick up their speech and avoid all other noise. They work well, but can limit the subject's freedom of movement if the microphone cable is connected directly to the camcorder. Reporters' microphones [1] are usually used in interview situations, and are simply held to the mouth of whoever is talking at the time. They only pick up sounds that occur close to them, and exclude background noise.

2

up close and personal

The best results in sound recording are achieved in bringing the microphone up close to the subject. This is rarely possible with the camcorder's built-in microphone, so an external mic is the only way to get clean close-up sound. Directional shotgun mics [2] should be held close in to the subject, just above the video frame. Angle the microphone down slightly, and point it straight at the speaker's mouth. Tie-clip mics [3] and reporters' microphones are designed specifically for close-up recording.

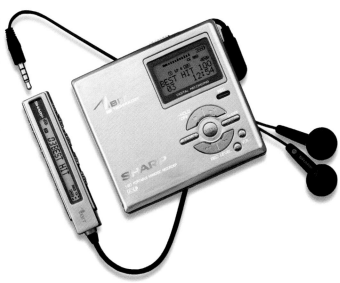

4

3

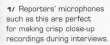

4/ Personal MiniDisc recorders can be useful as external sound recorders, especially when paired with tie-clip mics.

5/ Professional MiniDisc recorders are also available, with good level controls and balanced sockets for professional microphones.

1/ Reporters' microphones such as this are perfect for making crisp close-up recordings during interviews.

2/ Shotgun microphones are very directional, and can help achieve clean sound in situations where you can't get up close to the subject.

3/ Tie-clip microphones are a good compromise for close-up recording when you don't want a reporter's mic in shot – but trailing cables can limit your subject's freedom of movement.

external recorders

It is not always possible to have an external microphone connected directly to the camcorder. Take the case of a presenter held in a long shot and being filmed from the far side of a busy motorway – you can't point a shotgun mic across the road without picking up traffic noise,

and you can't stretch the cable from a tie-clip microphone across the road! The solution in this case is to use a separate sound recorder. Good results can be had by connecting a tie-clip mic to a personal MiniDisc recorder [4] and slipping it into the subject's jacket pocket. You'll need to sync

sound to picture later, however, so begin shooting by zooming in on the mic and having your presenter clap his or her hands in front of it to provide a visual and audible sync reference (in the same way that a clapper board is used for films).

wild tracks

Even though you've worked hard to eliminate background noise from your audio, you will still need some in the final edit. For this reason, you should always take time to record wild tracks.

what is a wild track?

Wild tracks are recordings of ambient background audio. For example, if you are shooting a movie at the seaside, your wild track might contain sounds of seagulls, waves crashing on rocks, or water lapping the sands. Video shot in a busy street market, however, might require a wild track depicting the general bustle of people as goods are bought and sold.

Wild tracks serve two important functions. First, they help give the impression that there is action going on outside the confines of the video frame. The careful addition of ambient noise adds depth and credibility to the scene. The fact that this audio has been recorded separately from the main sound provides control over its volume in the finished movie, making sure it doesn't overpower dialogue or other sound effects. Most importantly, the fact that wild track recordings are made in one long session means that background noise remains continuous and fluid in the final edit, even if you have been cutting back and forth between shots that were taken at different times. Wild tracks help make cuts seamless, resulting in a more natural, fluid video.

recording wild tracks

As with all sound recording, wild tracks benefit greatly from the use of a decent microphone. Recording the wild tracks themselves is easy – just connect a microphone to the camcorder and start shooting nothing in particular. The lens cap can even be on at this point, as you will only be interested in collecting sound. Make sure you monitor audio with a good pair of headphones, as recordings made to tape will sound very different to the way your brain interprets the live sound. Some environments, such as airports and shopping centres, don't like you shooting video at all. If you really need their ambient audio, be discreet about it by making your recording to a personal MiniDisc recorder rather than a camcorder. You should have no problems so long as the microphone is discreet!

Keep recordings running for a good few minutes, and be wary of any identifiable sounds (such as coherent speech or clock chimes). You may need to loop the sound during editing, and the repetition of specific noises will give the game away.

cheating with sound

There is no reason why wild tracks should be recorded at the same time and place as your main footage. Many movie-makers shoot small scenes in public places at quiet times, but come back later to collect more active background audio to create the impression that the scene is busier than it actually was. Some locations may be chosen for their good looks and clean acoustics, but lack any real dramatic tone. In this case, you may want to record wild tracks somewhere else entirely. Go for audio that sounds great and fits the mood you are trying to convey. Many film and TV productions even use pre-recorded CDs to provide ambient audio tracks such as 'hospital noise' or 'busy office'.

3

4

1/ Dedicated sound recorders can provide more control and versatility than a camcorder.

2/ Collecting wild tracks is essential for video involving lots of human voices, such as crowd and market scenes.

3/ Recording directly to the camcorder is the most convenient way to collect wild tracks.

4/ Be sure to collect audio from any mechanical elements that appear in frame.

be invisible

Video editing requires good judgement, experience and skill. The editor's importance in crafting and pacing a movie cannot be understated. But unlike artists in other fields, the editor's work should go unnoticed by the viewer.

the editor

As an editor, your job is to make a good movie a great one. That means choosing the best on-screen performances, and showing the camera crew and sound recordists at their best. It also means carefully pacing the movie to evoke the right emotional response and hold the audience's attention from start to finish. It is up to the editor to ensure that the movie makes sense, and that delivery of its message is effective and clear. Your audience should be absorbed in the movie itself,

remaining oblivious to the work that went into creating it. If a viewer notices the cutting, the photography, sound, lighting or effects, then their attention was probably wandering.

be the perfect guest

Homemade movies have a reputation for being unbearably dull, and the clichéd idea of guests politely enduring the ordeal of the annual holiday video is all too often a reality. Before inflicting your movie on another person, remember that, in this context, you are the guest. You are placing demands on the viewer's time, so make sure that it's worth it.

arrive late

Arriving early for a party can be awkward – especially if you are the very first guest and you weren't supposed to be there for another three hours. Similarly, your movie shouldn't take too long to get going. TV comedy and drama from the US provides the best example of quick-start production, with many shows delivering a short, high-impact introduction before the opening credits. Don't hang around waiting for introductions. Your audience should be able to catch up with the necessary gossip and backstory along the way.

keep things moving

Try to keep things moving smoothly. Don't let the party slow to a complete halt, as it might never get started again! Similarly, never stop the story for introductions and explanations. If it can't be explained on the move, something is seriously wrong.

The above rules of movie etiquette apply just as well to individual scenes as they do to a project as a whole. Always try to put yourself in the place of the viewer; keep the pace fluid, the message clear, and try not to be too self-indulgent.

leave early

Being the last person to leave a party can make you unpopular with your hosts, who are often tired and ready to call it a night, but have to politely wait around until you take the hint and go away! Know when your movie has said all it needs to say, and make your goodbyes short and sweet. There is no need to bolt out the door, but make an easy and elegant exit.

non-linear editing

the beginning

Long before the invention of video, there was film. Early film productions established a new language and technique that is still used with modern video technology. The process of shooting has always been similar for both formats, but editing methods were initially very different.

A film editor works with strips of celluloid that can be strung together in any number of combinations to create a narrative sequence. The way in which film prints are cut and joined allows changes to be made to a project at any time during post-production. Until quite recently, that versatility wasn't possible with video-editing technology. For many years, video was edited by copying picture and sound from one tape to another. A lot of sophisticated (and expensive) equipment was developed to make the process quick and accurate, but there was no avoiding the fact that each cut had to be right before the editor could move on. Any changes made to the middle of a programme would mean that everything after that point would have to be recut.

change

Non-linear video editing (NLE) was introduced to the professional world in 1989 with the first computer-based video editing systems from Avid. These systems allowed video and audio clips to be captured onto a Mac's hard drive, and then brought together in a sequence with all the versatility and control offered by film. Early systems were used to provide edit decision lists for tape-to-tape editors, but as computers became more powerful, and were able to handle higher quality media, the need for a final 'online' stage was virtually eliminated. Still, due to the high-end market of production companies with extravagant budgets, these early NLE systems were extremely expensive.

home users

The mid-1990s saw NLE join the mainstream, as home computers became more affordable. Companies such as Pinnacle Systems and Matrox were quick to launch 'affordable' hardware, allowing video to be captured to a computer's hard drive via analogue channels, and sent back out to tape the same way. Editing software such as Adobe Premiere was bundled to provide editing tools. On the whole, these systems worked well, but the hard drives needed to handle these video files were prohibitively expensive; many editors found problems keeping their editing systems stable with all the additional hardware they had installed; and there was also the problem of slight quality losses caused by capture via analogue video channels and the form of video compression used to squeeze footage to a more manageable size.

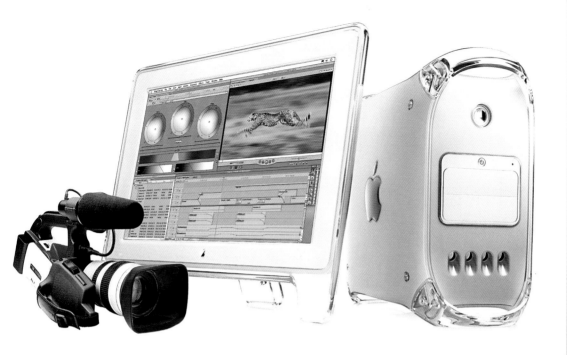

DV goes mainstream

While the launch of DV in 1995 was a huge boost for video photography, it took some years for the video editing market to really take advantage. The first generation of hardware and software for use with DV camcorders and their digital FireWire connections was often unstable and restrictive by today's standards. Hardware manufacturers managed to push stable DV capture cards into the mainstream towards the end of the 1990s, but, soon after, Microsoft and Apple introduced native DV and FireWire support into Windows and Mac operating systems. Today, all modern home computers are capable of handling digital video. And if a system isn't equipped with a FireWire port for interfacing with a camcorder, one can be added easily and cheaply.

Makers of editing software were once dependant on hardware manufacturers to integrate cutting tools with video capture and output channels. Today, a good variety of programs can be bought off-the-shelf confidently in the knowledge that they will work with your system for DV editing. Home computers are now very affordable, and boast more than enough power to handle a DV movie edit, and inexpensive modern hard drives are typically big enough and fast enough to handle quite sizeable DV editing projects. As for DV hardware manufacturers, they're still working hard to make you buy their capture cards, by boosting their performance in processing special effects, and including enticing bundles of software in-pack. The market is now mature, affordable and accessible. Best of all, there are inexpensive entry-level editing programs that offer richer editing features than the big, expensive tape-to-tape editing systems of yesteryear – all on your desktop!

1/ Within a decade, video editing computers have evolved from expensive, high-end systems to small and affordable desktop machines.

Just about any home computer today is powerful enough for DV editing [1]. Not all computers are ready to use as editors straight out of the box, however. Here is a breakdown of what you should expect to find in the most basic DV editing system.

DV editing systems

Hard drives

Hard drives [2] are used to store digital files (anything from video clips to simple text documents). DV video files are large and data-intensive: DV runs at 3.6 megabytes per second (MB/s), and an hour of footage requires about 13 gigabytes (GB) of hard-drive space. In the early years of desktop video production, appropriate hard drives were very expensive, but affordable drives are now available with capacities greater than 200GB and read/write speeds well in excess of 30MB/s. For good, smooth video-editing performance, it is strongly recommended that you invest in a second hard drive purely for video and audio files.

Processor

The computer's processor [3] handles all calculations and number-crunching. Processor speed is measured in Megahertz (MHz) or Gigahertz (GHz), but faster clock speeds are not always the most powerful. For Windows-based systems, Intel's processors have different strengths and weaknesses to AMD's, so a 2GHz Pentium processor may not give the same performance as a 2GHz Athlon. Much also depends on the rest of the system: slow hard drives, limited RAM, and a poor graphics card can all contribute

to a data bottleneck, slowing a system down regardless of how fast the processor is. Many systems designed for complex video editing and special effects have two processors rather than one.

Sound card

Sound cards [4] are responsible for processing audio. They feed the computer's speakers, but also provide inputs for sound recording – essential for recording audio commentaries or bringing in sound from MiniDisc or analogue tape. Many sound cards have surround-sound capabilities, and are able to cope with very high-resolution audio for studio recording or DVD Audio playback. This isn't an immediate requirement for the DV novice, but you should at least consider a surround-sound card if you plan to get involved in advanced DVD authoring.

RAM

RAM stands for Random Access Memory, and can be thought of as your computer's workspace [5]. The computer pulls files into the RAM while it works on them. Adding RAM to a system increases the amount of data that can be made available for processing at any one time. The speed of RAM chips is important, enabling the computer to access and file information as quickly as possible.

Graphics card

The graphics card feeds a visual signal to the computer monitor. A good graphics card will have a dedicated processor and memory chips on-board for processing graphics and video for display. Many advanced video editors use graphics cards with two monitor outputs, allowing them to spread their desktop over a greater area.

FireWire port

The FireWire port is also known as the i.Link port and the IEEE1394 interface. It is a standard connection for external devices, such as scanners, printers and external hard drives. It is also used for connecting DV camcorders, enabling digital transfer of DV footage to the system's hard drive. All current Mac computers have built-in FireWire ports. Many Windows-based PCs do too, and those that don't can have FireWire added with an inexpensive expansion card.

You will notice that the FireWire sockets on most computers are bigger than those on camcorders. Large six-pin connections are used for attaching devices that require power from the computer itself, such as external hard drives [6]. The smaller four-pin ports are used on devices that take their power from the mains. Your camcorder will most likely be connected to the computer

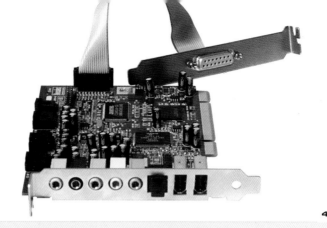

4

Editing software

Video-editing software is used to turn raw footage into a polished production. Video is captured to the system's hard drive via FireWire and then cut together. With the notable exception of Apple's iMovie, video-editing programs don't make any physical changes to your raw footage, and you can reverse any editing and effects decisions at any time. There are programs available to suit most budgets, from very affordable beginners' software to far more expensive applications for the pro market.

Camcorder or DV deck

DV camcorders or DV VCRs are used to feed video to the editing system and to record the finished edit to digital tape. The FireWire connection also allows playback to be controlled from the software application rather than having to work with one hand on the machine's physical controls.

Video monitor

Having a video monitor or small portable TV set handy is a good idea, as it provides a reliable representation of the movie in progress. If your editing software allows it, keep a camcorder or DV deck attached to the system via FireWire, and use it to channel the incoming DV feed out to your TV set.

The basics

A good comfortable mouse and keyboard are important for effective work. Your system should ideally be kitted out with a DVD-ROM drive, but a DVD burner would be even better for making DVD video copies of your finished movie. A fast internet connection is also advised for getting software updates quickly and easily. Treat yourself to a good set of speakers too!

1/ Computers may look daunting when you take the cover off, but they're little more than kits compiled from standard parts.

2/ A generous hard drive is a must for DV capture.

3/ The processor is responsible for much of a computer's number-crunching.

4/ A good sound card is useful for advanced projects with surround-sound.

5/ Computer RAM – make it abundant and fast!

6/ A six-pin FireWire port.

3

using a cable with a six-pin plug on one end and a four-pin plug on the other.

Monitor

The computer monitor is your display. A large monitor with a good clear image is a must, as you will be sitting looking at it for many hours at a time. Flat TFT monitors are falling in price, and they are worth considering, as they take up less desk space than normal monitors, produce less heat, and aren't prone to flicker. Stretching the desktop over two monitors can be a good idea when working with more advanced software.

6

KOREA A107
9450 FFF
HM5117400AS7

KOREA A107

5

Camcorder aside, a good modern home computer with a standard FireWire port and plenty of hard-drive space is all you really need to start editing video. But there is a huge market of advanced hardware devices out there that may become tempting as you become more ambitious.

1

DV editing hardware

DV decks

If you have chosen your camcorder carefully, it should work well as part of a DV editing set-up for video capture and output. More prolific editors might decide to invest in a dedicated DV VCR [1], however, which can remain permanently attached to the system. A DV deck might also be necessary if your camcorder doesn't have a working DV input. Several types of DV VCR are available, from small digital video Walkman decks to larger recorders with lots of sockets, and support for large-format tapes as well as MiniDV cassettes. They can all be controlled from the editing system, and provide real-time conversion between analogue and digital signals.

DV/AV converters

The biggest limitation of basic DV editing systems is that they don't provide a direct analogue video output for feeding a video monitor or recording directly to VHS tape. A good DV camcorder should serve this purpose well, but you might not want to have the camcorder attached to the system all the time while you are editing. A good solution comes in the form of small converter boxes that can convert between DV and analogue AV signals [2]. The most affordable options provide composite video and S-video input and output, while more advanced models have component video sockets for converting between DV and broadcast video formats, such as Beta SP.

Real-time editing boards

Video-editing programs are often packed with special effects. On basic systems, every special effect that is added to a movie will need rendering before it can be watched or recorded back to tape. Rendering simply means that the video clip with the effect is remade as a new file. Today's computers handle the workload quickly, but extensive use of effects such as colour correction can slow the editing process down considerably.

2

4

5

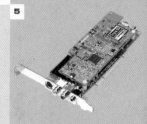

3

number of editing programs from beginners to professional levels. Sadly, those that opt for real-time hardware boards are restricted to editing their movies in specific programs. These programs will normally be provided with the card itself, but think carefully about what is most important to you – instant playback of fancy effects or freedom to choose the right editing software for your needs.

Real-time editing boards are expansion cards for the computer that provide instant playback of many special effects. They also take over the role of video capture and output, often providing analogue AV connections as well as a FireWire port for DV. Keep in mind that the most affordable real-time boards only provide instant output of effects via analogue video channels for viewing on a TV set, and they will still need to render your effects so they can be sent out via FireWire to DV tape. Only the more expensive real-time boards provide instant output via analogue and digital channels.

While a system using a simple FireWire port for capture and output might not have the benefit of real-time previewing of effects, it can be used with a huge

Hardware encoders

Once a movie is complete, it may need to be encoded into another format, such as MPEG for DVD authoring, or Windows Media for streaming on the internet. There are many ways to encode files in software, and most video-editing programs have built-in encoders for the most popular media formats. But, like special effects, the process can be time-consuming.

Hardware encoders typically come in the form of capture

devices (internal expansion cards or external boxes [4/5]), which bring in video via analogue audio and video channels, saving it to the hard drive in the required format. It is an immediate process, and results are normally excellent. Encoding hardware tends to support only one media format, however, so separate hardware encoders would be required for encoding to different file types, such as MPEG and Windows Media.

External drives

Laptops and small desktop computers such as Apple's iMac are seldom able to accommodate additional internal drives. External enclosures are available to house inexpensive EIDE devices [6]. They connect to the system via FireWire, and are immediately recognised by all current Mac and Windows operating systems.

1/ A small DV VCR.

2/ An analogue/digital converter.

3/ Standard OHCI FireWire ports provided by a simple expansion card.

4/ An external MPEG video encoder.

5/ An internal MPEG encoder.

6/ A FireWire enclosure for external drives.

6

1 Apple's iMovie

DV editing software

Regardless of how much money you have spent on dedicated DV hardware, most of your time will be spent working with software applications. There is a huge choice of DV editing programs, and they are all designed to work with basic FireWire connections on home computers. There is also a lot of good software for encoding video to other formats, and for creating DVD video presentations.

editing

Editing programs vary greatly in price, and it is not always the case that you get what you pay for [1/2/3]. At the very top of the price ladder are programs from high-end companies such as Avid. Their software is typically designed to work alongside their very expensive broadcast editing systems. Chances are that your movie won't be finished off on a Media Composer system, so there is no immediate need for you to go to that kind of expense.

There is some very poor software at the entry level, but other beginners' programs provide excellent editing tools, making some quite complex techniques easy and intuitive. Some drama and documentary projects may not need anything more than the tools provided by a good entry-level editor. Programs at all levels try to sell themselves on the strength of wild special effects, but the fundamental cutting tools are often overlooked in budget offerings. At the very least, a good beginners' program should provide a timeline-based interface with independent control over sound and picture. Accurate video trimming tools are a must too.

The most fierce competition lies with the more expensive prosumer software in the mid-range market. These programs –

2 Pinnacle's Edition

such as Adobe Premiere, Pinnacle's Edition, Ulead's MediaStudio Pro and Sonic Foundry's Vegas – provide immense levels of control over your movie, but can have a steep learning curve too. Understanding a program is always easier when you understand the job itself,

however, so don't be afraid to cut your teeth with affordable beginners' software first. By the time you need something more advanced, you will have a clear idea of how you like to work, and will be better able to decide which program is best for you.

3 Avid XPress DV

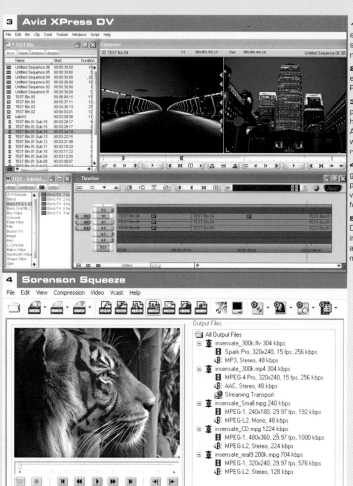

1/ Apple's iMovie is a good entry-level program. It is supplied as standard with most new Macs.

2/ Advanced Prosumer editing software in the form of Pinnacle's Edition DV.

3/ Expensive DV editing programs are provided by high-end companies such as Avid – but think carefully about whether the extra expense is really justified.

4/ Sorenson Squeeze is a good example of a single program designed to encode video to various different formats.

5/ Programs such as Ulead's DVD Workshop have been instrumental in pushing DVD authoring into the mainstream.

publishing

How will your movie be seen? All good editors allow finished videos to be sent back to tape, but publishing to DVD or VideoCD will often require additional authoring software. Recordable DVD is very affordable now, and there is already an impressive choice of authoring programs available for the beginner and enthusiast [5]. Multimedia authoring tools for making CD-ROM presentations can be inexpensive and user-friendly, but very few of the more accessible solutions are able to produce discs for playback on both Mac and Windows computers. Programs for integrating streaming video players into web pages are also in their infancy. In this case, some experience of hand-coding and programming is a definite bonus.

4 Sorenson Squeeze

File   Edit   View   Compression   Video   Vcast   Help

Output Files

All Output Files
- insensate_300k.flv 304 k.bps
  - Spark Pro, 320x240, 15 fps, 256 kbps
  - MP3, Stereo, 48 k.bps
- insensate_300k.mp4 304 k.bps
  - MPEG-4 Pro, 320x240, 15 fps, 256 kbps
  - AAC, Stereo, 48 k.bps
  - Streaming Transport
- insensate_Small.mpg 240 k.bps
  - MPEG-1, 240x180, 29.97 fps, 192 kbps
  - MPEG-L2, Mono, 48 k.bps
- insensate_CD.mpg 1224 k.bps
  - MPEG-1, 480x360, 29.97 fps, 1000 kbps
  - MPEG-L2, Stereo, 224 k.bps
- insensate_real9 200k.mpg 704 k.bps
  - MPEG-1, 320x240, 29.97 fps, 576 kbps
  - MPEG-L2, Stereo, 128 k.bps

sorenson media

Squeeze It   Vcast It

encoding

Most good editing programs allow movies to be exported in different media formats for DVD authoring, streaming on the web, or inclusion in multimedia projects. Results can vary, depending on the nature of the footage and the extent to which it is to be compressed. Programs such as Sorenson Squeeze [4], Discreet Cleaner and Canopus ProCoder provide additional media encoding tools. They can be expensive, but provide first-rate conversion to a variety of media formats. .

5 Ulead's DVD Workshop

organised editing

Video editing can be frustrating if you don't take the time to organise projects carefully. Basic librarianship skills are important for staying on top of all your footage and media files. Timecode is also a huge help in the quest for an easy, organised editing workflow. It was once found only in expensive professional video formats, but is now an integral part of the mainstream, being present in DV.

labels

Take a few moments to label tapes correctly, with date and contents on the inlay card, and a useful, meaningful title on the spine or face label. At the very least, the tape should tell you the event, date and location, and carry a number if more than one tape was shot on that occasion. Also, remember to flip the small tab on the right-hand side of the cassette's spine once the tape is full – this prevents accidental erasure. Establish a system for storing your DV cassettes too, so you always know where to find them, should a project need re-cutting.

00:09:16:19

00:09:17:00

00:09:17:07

00:09:17:14

00:09:17:21

00:09:18:03

1

indexing

Video-editing programs can be a great help in organising media if you know how to use them properly. Many programs provide logging tools for scanning and indexing tapes or captured video clips. This indexing can be related directly to captured media, allowing clips to be deleted and recaptured at a later date if necessary. Almost all editors allow you to rename video and audio files with sensible names. Some even provide a search feature to locate files by keyword. Another approach to organising media is the use of bins, allowing media to be divided between folders. A wedding video project, for example, might have separate bins for footage from the arrivals, ceremony, speeches and the reception.

1/ Outputting projects with burned-in timecode provides a useful reference for work in progress, allowing clients to identify exactly where they want to make changes.

2/ 3/ The process is the same for enthusiast programs such as Premiere as it is for professional applications like Avid XPress DV.

4/ Programs such as Vegas allow burned-in timecode displays to be added to video. This is useful when analysing rough cuts and work in progress.

timecode

Timecode is the numerical indexing of video frames. With DV video, each frame has its own unique code, presented in hours, minutes, seconds and frames. A frame occurring 23 minutes, four seconds and twelve frames into a recording would be coded as 00:23:04:12. Codes are unique to single frames on any given cassette providing timecode isn't accidentally reset to zero halfway through a tape.

Why use it?

Timecode allows accurate and reliable logging of shots recorded to DV tape. It also helps establish a close relationship between video footage captured to a system and the original tapes that they were

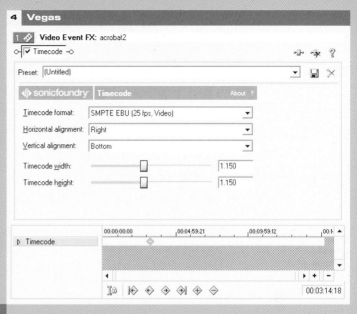

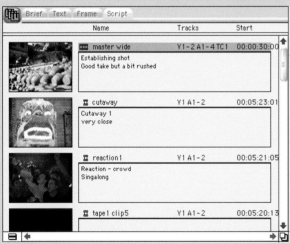

taken from. For example, some editing programs use timecode references as a guide during automated capture of several clips from a tape log. Others allow you to delete captured files (clearing space for other projects), and recapture them at a later date. Using the right editing software, any project can be rebuilt, providing the tapes are labelled correctly and their timecodes are unbroken.

Broken timecode

A broken timecode can cause problems at the editing stage, particularly when logging and capturing clips to the editing system. Timecode breaks occur when there are gaps of blank tape between shots, often as a result of removing tapes from the camcorder or previewing shots between takes. Timecode is often

reset to zero at timecode breaks too, meaning that there could be two or more sets of frames carrying the same timecode numbers. This makes accurate indexing very difficult and can confuse editing software during automated capture sessions.

Timecode breaks can be avoided by blacking tapes before a shoot. Simply putting the tapes into your camcorder and recording from beginning to end lays down a continuous timecode. Leave the lens cap on to produce a black image, and plug a headphone jack plug into the microphone socket to prevent any sound being recorded. That way, any gaps on the tape will be silent black video rather than candid chatter.

! *Draft quality capture* Pinnacle's entry-level editor, Studio, allows video to be captured in a highly compressed preview quality format. Preview quality files take up less space than DV video, allowing several hours' worth of material to be brought into the system without the need for a giant hard drive. Once the edit is complete, Studio will run a batch capture session, recapturing only the footage that you decided to use in the final movie, and rebuilding it at full DV quality.

! *Second hard drive* Having a second hard drive for captured video is far better than capturing to the same drive as your software and operating system. Data on system drives can become fragmented, slowing down access to video files. Also, if you allow the system drive to fill up completely, some programs may stop working properly, as they need space to create a cache of data. If you are using a laptop or an iMac that doesn't support a second internal hard drive, try using an external FireWire drive instead.

video capture

Before you can edit your video, it has to be captured to the editing system. Video capture used to be a complex job, in which an analogue video signal was converted into a digital format on its way into the system. However, the DV format and FireWire connections now mean that digital video information is simply copied from tape to hard drive, rather than being converted from one form to another.

device control

FireWire connections do more than carry digital video. They allow you to control a camcorder's playback and record functions from the computer software. This bridges a big gap between hardware and software, allowing you to do all your work with the editing software, without the need to keep one hand on the camcorder. In this example [1], we are controlling a camcorder from within Ulead's VideoStudio.

detection

Timecode isn't the only data to be saved to DV tape. Recordings also store the time and date that they were made. A sudden change indicates that recording was paused, and a new scene is beginning, prompting some editors to split incoming video, dividing long captures into smaller, more manageable, chunks. This scene detection process [2] can also be made to respond to sudden changes in picture or sound. This is useful if your DV video has been copied from an analogue source.

1 VideoStudio control panel

2 scene detection

logging

Some programs scan tapes and create logs of scenes based on changes in date and time stamp. Each scene is given a thumbnail icon of its first frame, and can be renamed and annotated as required. Logging applications such as this are valuable for providing an immediate reference to all your video material for a project, and the scene can then be selected for capture at any time [3].

1/ VideoStudio 7 provides full control over connected DV camcorders and digital VCRs. It also enables basic batch capture and even allows video to be captured directly into MPEG or streaming video formats.

2/ Scene detection tools as provided by VideoStudio 7 allow clips to be split by date and time stamp, or by on-screen content. Captured video can be split manually too.

3/ Scenalyzer has excellent tape logging, scene detection and capture tools. It even allows tapes to be scanned and logged in fast forward, taking only five minutes to log a 60-minute tape!

4/ Batch capture tools in Sonic Foundry's Vegas provide the means to name clips, as well as add comments and rate clips as good, bad or excellent.

5/ Premiere's batch capture tools also allow the addition of comments to captured files.

3 | tape logging

4 | Vegas' batch capture

5 | Premiere's batch capture

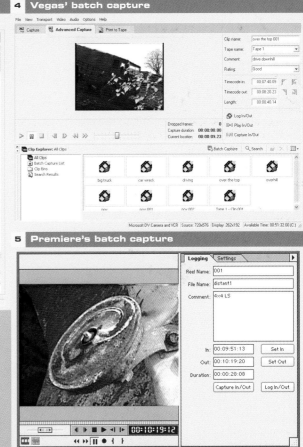

batch capture

Timecode and device control make batch capture a possibility for DV projects [4/5]. Logged clips are selected for capture (either with a dedicated logging tool or by manually marking timecode references for the start and end of clips you want to use). The selected video files are then captured to the system in one session, with the computer handling playback of the camcorder to locate the appropriate timecode references. Batch capture can normally be left unattended unless the batch spans several cassettes, in which case the system will ask you to change tapes every now and then.

DV sound control It is important to be able to cut a video file's picture and sound independently. Some entry-level programs won't allow you to do this, even if they have a timeline interface. Before buying an editor, check that its timeline provides direct access to the audio element of your DV footage. If it doesn't, you won't be able to perform some of the more seamless editing techniques, such as audio splitting (see page 77).

A second video track A second video track will allow you to overlay one video clip onto another; this is useful for adding illustrative cutaways or graphics. Some beginners' editors won't allow this, so take care. On the

storyboards and timelines

There are two common types of video-editing interface: storyboards and timelines. Some editing programs provide a choice between the two, but others are restricted to only one or the other.

storyboards

Storyboards provide a very simple environment for assembling video clips in sequence. Clips are represented as thumbnail icons, all of a uniform size, regardless of their duration [1/2]. While the process provides an immediate representation of the movie's construction, storyboards don't allow any direct access to a movie's sound, and don't allow more complex (and important) editing techniques, such as assemble editing or audio splitting (see pages 76–77). Many programs, even at professional levels, offer storyboards for very quick assembly of sequences, but

1 iMovie storyboard

2 Studio storyboard

experienced editors prefer to do most of their work in a timeline interface, which provides much more control.

1/ 2/ Simple storyboard editing in Apple's iMovie and Pinnacle's Studio.

3/ 4/ Timelines in the same entry-level applications. Notice that the duration of clips is represented, as is audio.

5/ Professional editors, such as Pinnacle Edition, have very advanced timelines for complex cutting.

6/ 7/ Good professional and prosumer editors have trimming windows, allowing accurate fine-tuning of edit points on the timeline.

trimmers

Edit trimmers are used to fine-tune the position of cuts on the timeline. They are composed of two video displays, showing the last frame of one clip, and the first frame of the next [6/7]. Trimming controls allow the cutting points of individual clips to be taken in or let out one frame at a time. Alternatively, the last and first frames of

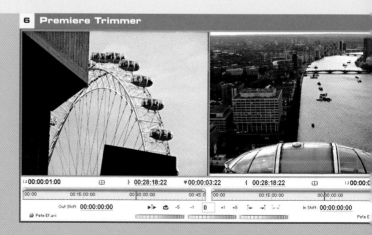

6 Premiere Trimmer

other hand, some other beginners' programs provide separate tools for overlaying footage. This is not as convenient or versatile as a second video track, but is useful nonetheless.

3 Studio timeline

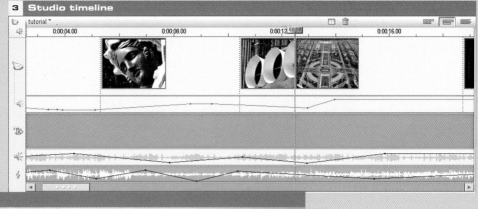

4 iMovie timeline

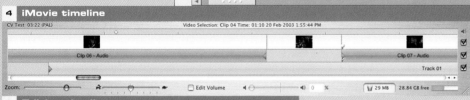

5 Edition timeline

timelines

A timeline enables video and sound clips to be arranged on parallel layers called tracks [3/4]. A time-scale runs along the timeline's horizontal axis, and long clips occupy more space than shorter ones. This alone gives a better representation of a movie's pacing than you would get from a storyboard. Most importantly, timelines represent sound as well as video, providing good control over audio mixing, and allowing DV video and sound to be cut at different times for insert and split edits. Well-featured prosumer editing programs often provide an unlimited number of video and audio tracks, which can be used for complex compositing effects and rich sound mixes [5].

adjacent clips at an edit point can be altered simultaneously – keeping both clips in the same relative position, but moving the position of the cut itself. This latter approach is ideal for fine-tuning cuts of live events shot with multiple cameras, where the footage has been carefully synced in advance. Trimming windows are extremely useful, but are normally found only in prosumer and professional-level software.

7 Edition Trim

multiple video tracks

Advanced editors allow you to work with many video tracks at once. This allows compositing such as picture-in-picture, superimposition or transparency effects, but can also be useful when editing live events shot with multiple cameras – syncing all video and audio on the timeline before you start cutting [1]. As with layers in photo-editing programs, the uppermost video track is the one that is visible, unless a transparency effect is applied to allow lower tracks to show through.

advanced timeline tools

The timelines of advanced **DV** editing programs have special features to help organise and navigate complex projects. They can also provide easy access to commonly used effects tools.

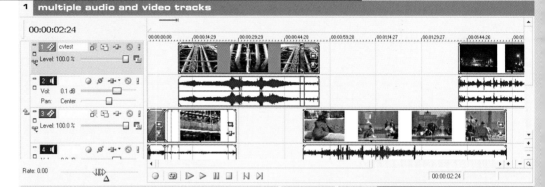

1 multiple audio and video tracks

enable/disable and mute

Next to timeline tracks on all advanced editing programs, you'll find a simple button to turn that track on and off. On a video track, this makes the picture invisible, allowing footage in lower tracks to be seen instead. It's important to get used to toggling tracks on and off, especially when working with complex effects sequences.

In the case of audio, the enable/disable buttons serve to mute that particular track [2]. This is important when concentrating on background effects or music, but can also be valuable if you need to work with several versions of the soundtrack, such as commentaries in different languages.

2 enable and disable

sync lock

When you add video to the timeline of an advanced editing program, the clip's audio will normally appear separately on its own audio track. Despite the apparent separation, any adjustments made to the position and trimming of the picture will also affect the sound. There are occasions, however, when you'll want to edit picture and sound separately – if you want to cut them at different times, or you deliberately want to pull the sound out of sync, or just remove the sound altogether. In all cases, a 'sync-lock' control will be provided, allowing you to break the tie between video and audio, then re-establish it again when necessary.

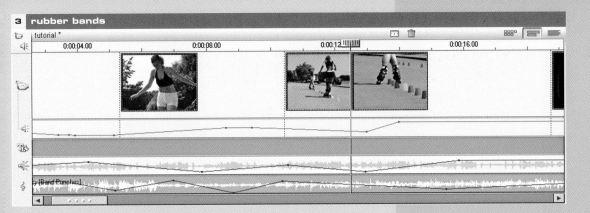

razor

Razors provide an easy way to split clips on the timeline. The tool is useful for quick cutting back and forth between your main video and cutaways or reaction shots. It's often possible to slice through all video and audio clips at a given point of the timeline – ideal for cutting live multi-camera events in which several video clips have been stacked up at the start.

rubber bands

Rubber bands are an intuitive and tactile method of adjusting levels – most commonly sound levels on audio tracks [3]. The rubber band is a visible bar on the timeline, which can be dragged upwards to increase the audio level, or brought down to decrease it. These levels can also be made to change over time, by making changes between points called keyframes. Rubber bands are also used by some programs to control transparency of the picture on video tracks (see page 81).

1/ Multiple video tracks can be used to facilitate the editing of live events where more than one camera has been used.

2/ Use enable and disable buttons to mute a particular audio track.

3/ Rubber bands can be used to adjust sound levels.

4/ Sequences and nests are valuable for organising large-scale projects.

sequences and nests

Large projects composed of numerous scenes can be difficult to manage, and editing a long movie from start to finish as a single sequence can make it difficult to remove or re-order scenes later. Many good editors allow you to cut each sequence separately on its own timeline, then combine them into a new sequence of their own – with timelines 'nested' within other timelines [4]. Not only is this a good way of organising big productions, but it provides excellent control over individual scenes and the overall movie.

! *Naming tracks* If your editor allows it, take the time to assign names to video and audio tracks. This is especially important for complex sound edits, allowing you to allocate specific tracks for dialogue, commentary, music and effects.

! *Picture icons* Some editors allow you to control the 'look' of video clips on the timeline. Presenting video as a strip of thumbnail images is a useful tool for locating specific scenes when moving back and forth in the project, although it can slow down performance on more modest systems.

! *Cutaways* A cutaway is a close-up shot of any key prop or detail that might feature in a scene. It can be anything from a glass being filled to a key being turned in a lock. It's important to shoot as many as possible, even if you don't use them all. Cutaways are invaluable for subtly shortening scenes that run too long or adding interest to potentially dull and 'talky' footage. Many low-budget productions schedule whole days for shooting cutaways, while larger productions hire whole film units to film such details.

! *Reaction shots* Reaction shots are used in much the same way as cutaways, but serve to show how a scene affects the people within it. When editing the best man's speech at a wedding reception, some carefully placed shots of guests laughing will help you show that his speech was humorous and entertaining. Reactions of the bride, groom or immediate family, will evoke the sense of pride or even embarrassment that such a speech might evoke. And, like cutaways, they provide a cover should you need to remove unwanted hesitation, repetition and 'ums' and 'ahs'.

editing basics

A simple sequence of video clips butted end-to-end might serve to tell a story, but you're unlikely to achieve the level of fluidity and sleekness of pacing that a good movie needs. At the very basic level, it's important to remember that you're dealing with two types of media here – pictures and sound – and that they can be cut independently of each other. Editing captured video footage relies on three basic techniques – assemble editing, insert editing and audio splitting.

1 assemble

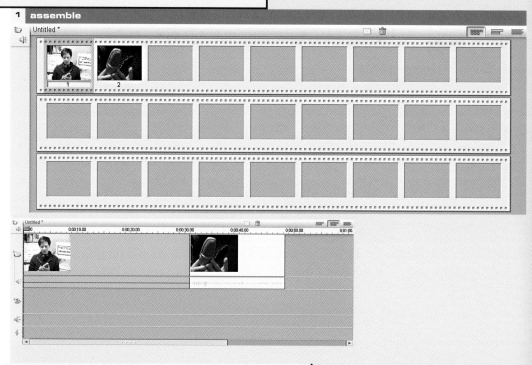

assemble editing

Assemble editing is the process of joining video clips end-to-end, with sound and picture cut at exactly the same time – not very different to the effect had when you pause and resume recording on a home VCR. This is the simplest method of constructing an edited sequence, but also the least elegant. However, many editors use assemble editing to storyboard their project and lay the foundations before returning and tidying up with inserts and audio splitting. The examples above [1] show assemble editing in Pinnacle's Studio 8 using storyboard and timeline views. As we continue through the next examples, notice how the relationship between video and sound tracks differs from this basic cut.

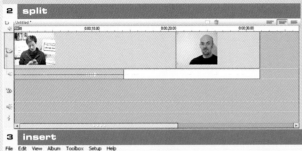

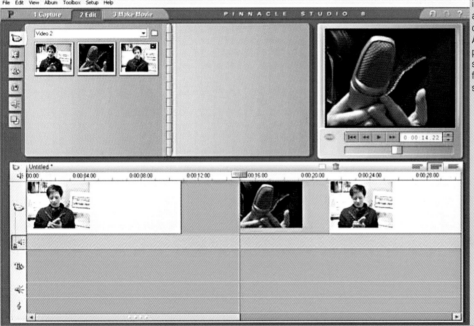

Put simply, audio splitting is a process of cutting sound and picture at different times [2]. After shooting this interview, we turned our camera on the interviewer and made him repeat all his questions (and fake a few nods and interested reactions as if the interviewee were still talking). The interviewer's questions could be crudely cut in and out of the video with assemble editing techniques, but it's far more elegant to cut picture and sound separately. Naturally, sound for the next question can't be cut in until the interviewee has finished answering the one before, but the picture can. If we cut to a nodding reaction shot just prior to the next question being asked, we create the illusion that two cameras were in use, and that both shots were taken at the same time. The screengrab here shows audio splitting performed in Pinnacle's Studio 8. Notice how audio and video cuts occur at different positions on the timeline. As with insert editing, split editing provides another means to seamlessly trim unwanted footage from a movie and keep it flowing smoothly.

1/ Assemble editing as seen on a storyboard and timeline interface. Notice how picture and sound cut at exactly the same time.

2/ A split edit: In this case, sound is cut before the picture to create a sense of interruption.

3/ Insert editing facilitates the insertion of cutaways that can help a movie flow more smoothly.

insert editing

Insert editing [3] enables a section of video to be replaced with another without disturbing its audio. In the above example, we're cutting an interview with an audio technician. She's talking about some of the microphones used on location, and we wanted to add a close-up of one of these mics to illustrate this. With assemble editing, we'd have to stop the dialogue to edit in the close-up, but a simple insert edit allows us to overwrite a portion of the original interview footage, leaving the sound in place. Insert editing allows illustrative 'cutaways' to be used without disturbing the flow of the final movie, but it also provides a means to subtly remove material without anyone noticing. We can't just remove part of the single-camera interview without the audience seeing an obvious jump in the subject's facial expression or position. Introducing a cutaway at the join allows us to truncate the footage and remove any stutters, hesitation or repetition without anyone noticing.

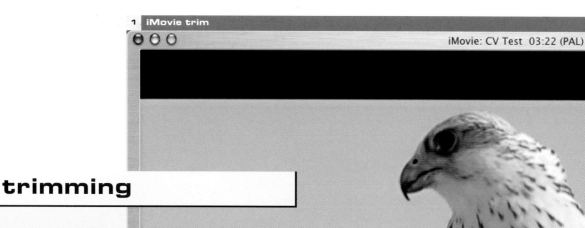

iMovie: CV Test 03:22 (PAL)

23:03

trimming

It is good practice to capture a little more footage than you need, rather than run the risk of finding yourself short of material. It is likely that captured video files will need breaking down into smaller chunks before they can be added to an edited sequence. This process is known as trimming.

! **Trimming on a timeline**
Most good editing programs allow further trimming after footage has been sent to the timeline. Simply clicking the edge of a clip and pulling left or right allows you to tighten the edit or let it out. Most advanced editors also provide a trimming window providing control over how a cut leads from one clip to the next.

tops & tails

Most captured video clips have excess footage at the beginning and end that must be removed in order for the edited sequence to run quickly and smoothly. The procedure for removing unwanted tops and tails is the same for all editing programs [1/2]: the file is opened in a viewer window, sporting playback controls and a scrubbing bar with which you can move forward and back through the clip by dragging the mouse left and right. These controls are used to navigate the file to the frame at which the clip is to start, then a mark-in button is clicked to select it as the new beginning.

2 studio trim

Name: Video 1 [1:36.22]   Duration: 0:00:05.05

0:00:00.00

[0:00:00.00]   [0:00:05.04]

The same process is followed in locating the desired end frame. Some editors provide handles on the scrubbing bar to denote in and out points. These cutting decisions are normally applied automatically – the main exception being Apple's iMovie, which requires confirmation in the form of a crop command.

! | _Destructive iMovie_ Non-destructive editors allow you to make changes to an edit without making any actual changes to the video files themselves. This accounts for most **DV** editing programs, and it is a good approach, allowing decisions to be reversed at any time if you don't like the way a movie is turning out. Apple's iMovie does things differently, however. Trimming a video file splits up the file itself, sending the unwanted tops and tails to a trash bin. If you have trimmed too much from the clip, it must be restored to its original length and trimmed again (other editors will allow you to let it out a frame at a time if necessary). If the trash bin has been emptied since trimming the clip, all tops and tails will be lost, and the mistake can't be corrected. You'll have to capture that clip again!

sub-clips

Long video captures may contain material that you plan to divide up and use at different stages of the movie. To help keep track of what is where, it helps to split them up into sub-clips before editing begins. Advanced editing programs, such as Pinnacle Edition have dedicated tools for marking sub-clips. Other editors may require files to be copied, while some entry-level programs allow sub-clips to be created with scene detection tools.

In Edition: use the clip viewer [3] to mark a portion of the file with in and out points as you would if

you were removing unwanted tops and tails. This time, instead of sending the trimmed clip directly to the edit, click on the Make Sub-clip icon. A new file icon appears in Edition's clip bin, representing the newly trimmed file. Edition hasn't created a new DV file on the hard drive, just made reference to your trimming decisions with a virtual file that can be renamed, played and edited like any other video.

In Premiere [4/5]: Highlight the clip that needs to be divided. From the Edit menu, select Copy. Now use Paste to duplicate the clip in the project

window – once for each sub-clip you intend to make. No actual data has been duplicated on the hard drive, so there is no need to worry about hard drive space at this point. Trim each instance of the clip as you would any other video file.

1/ Topping and tailing in Apple's iMovie. Note the yellow section of the scrubbing bar, indicating which part of the clip will be used.

2/ The same process in Pinnacle's Studio. In this case, trimming takes place after a clip has been added to the timeline.

3/ Sub-clips are made in Edition's clip viewer. The highlighted button on the control panel is used to add a virtual sub-clip to the project window.

4/ 5/ Sub-clips in Premiere are made by simply copying and pasting icons in the project window. Each one can be topped and tailed in the monitor window as if it were a real video file on the hard drive. Notice the dark grey area on the scrubbing bar denoting the portion of video that has been selected for the edit.

3 Edition's clip viewer

! Cut to the beat Editors that display a visible waveform on their audio tracks make editing to music a breeze. The waveform shows where beats fall, and helps you cut to the audio rhythm without having to rely purely on ear/hand coordination!

! Music copyright Before you dig into your record collection to provide music for a movie, be aware that you will almost certainly be breaking copyright law if you use it. This may not be a huge deal if you are making a movie just for yourself, but any commercial projects such as wedding videos or training videos should have music rights cleared if

you want to stay on the right side of the law. A few companies specialise in producing copyright assigned CDs with short (and often very bland) audio links for your project. Alternatively, programs such as Sonic SmartSound can help generate musical links to your specification of style and tempo, and will snugly fit the required duration.

sound editing

Good sound is essential for good video. Take care over your movie's soundtrack and be as creative with audio as you are with your visuals. Good use of sound can make cuts invisible, enhance mood, and completely change the feel of your movie's location.

1 Edition mixer

mixing

An edited movie will probably contain live audio from your DV footage, incidental music, and – if you have done a thorough job – a wild track. If the project is a documentary or training video, you might also decide to record a commentary. All these sounds are positioned easily on a timeline, but some care must be taken to ensure that they are correctly balanced. Some editors have a mixer interface, which resembles a physical sound desk with sliders to control audio levels (or loudness) for each track. These three examples show the mixers in Pinnacle's Edition [1], Ulead's MediaStudio Pro [2] and Adobe Premiere [3]. In

2 MediaStudio Pro mixer   **3 Premiere mixer**

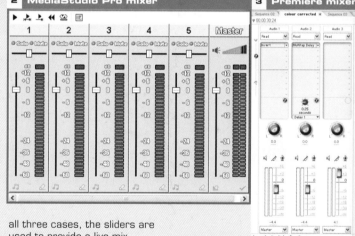

all three cases, the sliders are used to provide a live mix, increasing and decreasing the audio level of tracks as the movie plays back.

1/ 2/ 3/ The mixer interfaces in these three programs have been designed to resemble actual sound desks complete with control sliders.

4/ 5/ Using rubber bands to control audio levels in MediaStudio Pro and Final Cut Pro.

6/ Commentary recording in Pinnacle's Studio.

7/ Sound level monitoring in Vegas.

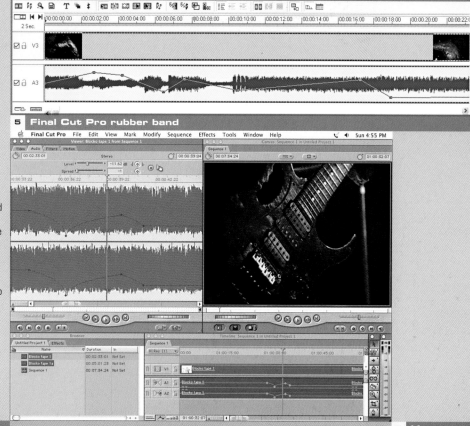

4 MediaStudio Pro rubber band

5 Final Cut Pro rubber band

rubber bands

Rubber bands provide a visual and tactile representation of audio levels on the timeline. They enable very accurate adjustment of sound levels, such as dipping music just in time for dialogue to come in. These examples show rubber bands used in MediaStudio Pro [4] and Final Cut Pro [5].

6 Studio commentary

7 Vegas

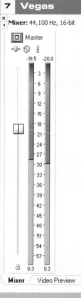

Monitoring sound Computer speakers can sound very different from a TV set. If your movie is designed for watching on TV rather than a computer, try to monitor picture and sound on a small portable TV or video monitor rather than relying on the computer to give you an accurate representation of the work in hand.

commentary

Commentary recording tools are most commonly found in entry-level programs such as Pinnacle's Studio [6]. Voiceovers are recorded through a microphone directly to the timeline while the movie plays back. Some advanced programs, such as Vegas, allow you to make several takes of the commentary, recording again and again in a loop until you are confident that one of the takes is useful.

levels

If material is coming from different sources, recorded under different conditions, you may find some big differences in the loudness of dialogue from one clip to the next. Audiences generally expect speech to remain at a constant level throughout a production, so take care with sound levels to retain a sense of continuity throughout. Never allow background music or wild tracks to overshadow dialogue either, and monitor the overall level of your movie's audio when it is all mixed together [7]. You want a good dynamic range of sound in your project, and mixing several sources can push overall audio levels up quite high.

! **Split screen** Transition effects don't always have to take the audience from one clip to the next. Advanced video-editing programs allow you to position wipe effects at a halfway point, creating a split-screen effect.

! **Reference photos** Dissolves can be more effective if the incoming and outgoing video clips are framed in much the same way. For example, you may want to keep the horizons in the same place when dissolving between landscapes. Camcorders with still image capabilities are a great help in lining up such shots. After shooting one clip, take a still photo on the camcorder's memory card. When framing the next shot, use the camcorder's special effects tools to superimpose the still image on top of the video image, providing an accurate source of reference. Once the two are lined up, disable the overlay effect and start shooting!

subtle transitions

Transition effects provide a slow change from one shot to the next. There are many different types of transition. Editing programs sometimes come with more than a hundred as standard, but most are so wild and wacky that they divert the viewer's attention away from the movie rather than helping to drive it along. Some restraint and focus is useful when you start to play with video effects. Is your choice of transition appropriate to the video, or did you just choose it because it looks cool?

transitions

Transition effects such as fades [1], wipes [2], and dissolves [3] often signify a change of time or place. If you look closely at the editing of documentaries and dramas on TV, you will see that fades and dissolves aren't used in the middle of dialogues or interviews – doing so would detract from the immediacy of the scene. Instead, they are used primarily to lead the viewer into a different scene altogether. Transitions aren't essential for scene changes, though. Many movie-makers prefer more subtle and creative techniques, such as using cutaways or sound cues common to both scenes – possibly giving the impression that a conversation is continuing across two scenes with different players. You will often find that the more well-crafted a movie is, the fewer transition effects are necessary.

Applying transitions

In most timeline-based editing programs [4/5/6/7], transitions are dropped between adjacent tracks. Transition settings allow you to specify a duration for the effect (provided there is enough video on either side of the cut to accommodate it), and set wipe direction if necessary. Ulead's MediaStudio Pro allows video to be compiled on two tracks with a separate track in between specifically for transition effects. In this case, clips are arranged on separate tracks, with a transition effect between them in an overlapping area.

1/ 2/ 3/ Fades, wipes and dissolves are effective and subtle transitions.

4/ Transitions appear as self-contained icons between clips in storyboard-based editors.

5/ MediaStudio Pro divides its main video track into two, allowing transition effects to be dropped in between.

6/ 7/ Transitions are often dropped between adjacent clips on a timeline, as seen here with iMovie and Final Cut Pro.

fade

A fade [1] is the gradual appearance or disappearance of picture. It is an effect similar to slowly closing or opening the camcorder's iris. Many movies begin with a fade-in from a black frame, and end with a fade-out to black. The effect is very natural in this context, but should be handled with care when used mid-movie. Fading to black stops everything dead and can badly disrupt the project's overall flow. A simple cut from one scene to the next might be better for maintaining the movie's momentum than allowing it to fade to black.

dissolve

Dissolves [3] are similar to fades, but instead of fading from video to a black frame, there is a slow change from one clip to the next. It is as if a fade-out and fade-in are happening simultaneously. As with most transitions, dissolves should be avoided mid-scene, but they often provide a good and natural way to move to a new one. The basic cross-dissolve is one of the most discreet transition effects, as it adds interest to the frame without drawing too much attention to itself.

4 iMovie storyboard editor

5 MediaStudio Pro editor

6 iMovie timeline editor

7 Final Cut Pro

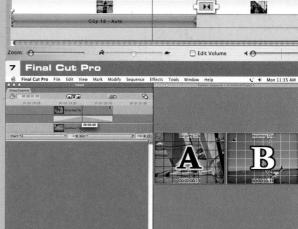

wipe

As the name suggests, wipes [2] are effects in which one image is wiped away, leaving another beneath. The shape of the wipe edge can be a straight line, circle, rectangle, or something far more extreme, such as smoke or spirals. In most cases, wipes are more conspicuous than dissolves, but a little creativity can result in some beautifully seamless transitions between scenes. Moving shots are open to some very discreet wipe transitions particularly if the frame is ever obscured by dark objects, such as walls, pillars, or even people. Wiping with foreground motion provides an almost seamless transition, giving the impression that no cuts have been made at all.

> **! _Rendering_** Unless you're using good real-time hardware in your editing system, you'll probably find that any of the changes listed here will need to be rendered before they can be previewed properly on an external monitor or sent out to tape. Modern desktop computers can render special effects very quickly, but be prepared for a lot of waiting if you're determined to thoroughly 'grade' long projects.

colour correction

Perhaps the most important type of video effect available to the DV editor is colour correction. Makers of theatrical movies and big-budget TV shows will spend some time 'grading' their movie once it has been cut. Grading is a process in which colour, tone and contrast are adjusted to help create a specific feel. The same kind of tools are available to DV movie-makers. They can greatly enhance a movie, create a stylistic effect or correct mistakes such as incorrect white balance.

presets and controls

Some editing programs, particularly those at the entry level, provide simple ready-made settings to make footage appear warmer, cooler, or to apply more stylistic effects such as black and white or sepia tone.

This example shows a range of options provided by Roxio's VideoWave [1]. There are many cases where presets will provide a good effect and avoid the need to play with individual image properties and more

controlled work will require a good understanding of how specific controls affect a video image. Advanced editors such as Final Cut Pro [2] provide a good comprehensive selection of image controls.

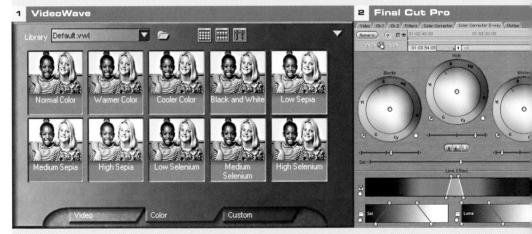

> **! _Monitoring_** It's likely that you've been previewing your edits on the computer monitor until now. For colour correction, however, it's useful to examine changes on an external video monitor or TV set if your editing software allows it. For systems with no analogue AV outputs, feed the video to your camcorder or deck via FireWire, and allow it to convert it to an analogue signal for viewing on a TV set.

brightness and contrast

Anyone with a TV set should be familiar with the idea of brightness and contrast controls. Making a change to brightness levels alters the amount of black or white within an image. Increasing the brightness might help expose lost detail in the shadows, but can also result in a rather hazy feel, with poor contrast and a loss of detail in the highlights [3].

Contrast controls the range of tones that provide an image with its shading. A slight increase in contrast will almost always make footage appear more dramatic, and will help make pale, washed-out video look more dynamic. Boosting contrast too much will result in a loss of detail in shadows and highlights, however, and give a very stylised and unnatural effect.

hue and saturation

Most editors provide sliders to control the hue, saturation and 'lightness' of an image. Altering the 'hue' moves all colours in the image along the spectrum [4]. As the spectrum of colours exists as a wheel rather than a linear gradient, you'll find that the furthest extremes of a hue slider give the same result.

Saturation sliders simply alter the overall intensity of colour within an image. If the picture appears washed out, boosting saturation can help make things appear more vibrant. Similarly, a drop in saturation can help evoke a more oppressive and downbeat quality.

Lightness controls adjust the amount of white or black in the picture, and serve a very similar purpose to brightness controls.

3

4

5 effect controls

1/ Roxio's VideoWave provides simple preset options for enhancing colour.

2/ Advanced controls in programs such as Apple's Final Cut Pro are comprehensive but potentially intimidating.

3/ The effect of increasing brightness and boosting contrast.

4/ Adjusting hue can result in subtle tonal changes or have an extreme and unnatural effect.

5/ Individual control over red, green and blue channels can produce some interesting results.

the primaries

The video image is composed of three channels, each accommodating a primary colour – red, green and blue. Many editing programs provide the means to alter the intensity of each primary colour independently of the others [5]. A slight drop in the level of blue can help warm up an image slightly, while a drop in reds can help produce a more 'icy' feel. Losing one or two channels altogether produces an odd, stylised image, which can prove useful for abstract edits such as title sequences or DVD menus. Try experimenting with different settings, but remember that very small adjustments are often all you need!

! Keep it relevant Wild effects can be great fun, but they draw a lot of attention to your influence as an editor and often detract from the movie itself. Eccentric alpha wipes and 3D transitions can be right at home in some corporate productions and magazine-type programmes but, even then they can become annoying if overused.

! Rendering times Unless you're using real-time hardware on your system, any effect you add to a project will require rendering before it can be played back. Some real-time solutions still require effects to be rendered before they can be sent out to **DV** tape via **FireWire**. The longer and more complex an effect is, the more time it takes to render.

1/ 2/ A simple gradient wipe transition. Note how the effect follows the gradient path from white to black.

3/ Complex transition editors are available to customise complex 3D transition effects.

4/ Page peels are among the most popular of fancy 3D transitions.

5/ 3D transition effects can be as wild as you like, with particle effects such as this 'shatter' transition.

wild transitions

Most video-editing programs provide a vast selection of 'wild' transition effects. You might not need to use any of them, but for many people, the temptation is too great and they go further and buy more in the form of ready-made packs or software kits to help them design their own transition effects. Wild transitions won't necessarily make your video any better (and they could ruin it completely), but if you have to play...

gradient wipes

Gradient wipes [1/2] use black-and-white image files to provide a shape, direction and speed for wipe effects. A gradient wipe would begin in the lightest areas of the image and progress to the darkest. The shape of the gradient represents the shape of the wipe edge; the direction of the gradient decides the direction of the wipe; and the rate of tonal

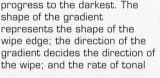

change within the bitmap image affects its speed. A typical example is a clock wipe, which sweeps round in a circle from the centre of the frame. More creative wipes include smoke and dripping paint effects. Packages such as Pixelan's Spice Rack are available with hundreds of ready-made gradients. You can also create your own gradients for these programs using image-editing tools such as Adobe Photoshop.

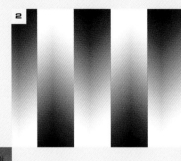

editors

Effects fanatics may well find themselves investing in transition editors such as Boris FX or Pinnacle's Hollywood FX [3]. These are plug-in programs that work alongside video-editing software, allowing you to create fancy transitions from scratch. Basic templates can be edited and enhanced, with excellent control over lighting effects on 3D shapes and motion blur. Complex transitions can be keyframed on a timeline, allowing you to decide how long each stage of the effect will take. Transition editors such as this provide excellent levels of control, but they can be expensive and complicated to use. Be absolutely sure that you need these types of effects before you surrender a lot of time and money.

3D effects

3D transitions are among the most dynamic and impressive effects available in mainstream editing software. They allow a video clip to take on a three-dimensional form (such as a ball or paper aeroplane) and exit the frame, leaving a new clip in its place. A typical example is the page peel effect, in which one video clip peels away to reveal another behind it [4]. More elaborate variations include shatter effects [5], in which the outgoing video explodes like shattered glass, and cube spins, in which video clips are displayed on different faces of a rotating cube.

image filters

before applying these filters. One popular type of effect is the 'old film' filter, which makes your bright, clean video look like scratched and beaten 8mm cine-film [2]. Other filters apply texture to the image, making the video look as if it has been shot through frosted glass, for example. There is no end to the variety of effects that can be created with filters [3], from subtle to extreme, and they are easy to apply [4].

! *More rendering* **Even real-time effects boards have their limits. Many can only handle one or two video filters in real-time, and combinations of three or more will still require rendering.**

Unlike transition effects, which lead from one video clip to another, video filters are applied to the clips themselves to change their appearance. Some, like colour correction effects, can be subtle and discreet, while others are more stylised and often just plain silly.

artistic filters

Artistic filters are designed to emulate the look of an artistic medium such as watercolour, pencil drawing or mosaic. How well they work depends greatly on the nature of the original footage [1]. Most result in a loss of detail, and some provide better results with very high-contrast images. Try adjusting the movie's brightness, contrast and sharpness to emphasise form and reduce the tonal range

2 old film filter

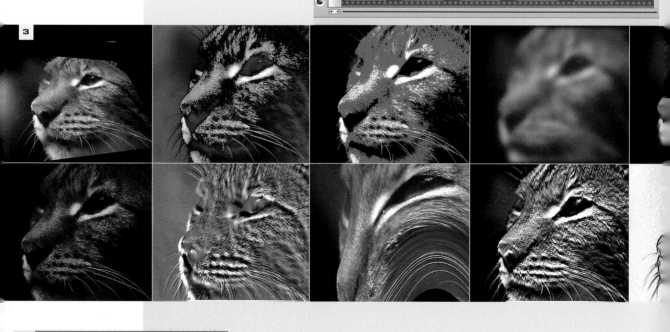

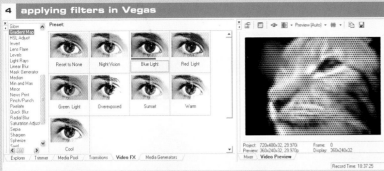

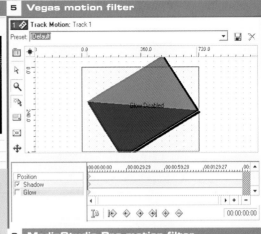

motion

Motion filters allow movement of photos or videos within the frame. While it can be fun to have a video image fly around the screen, the effect really comes into its own when used with still photos. High-resolution image files can have details enlarged without the loss of quality that results from zooming into a video image. Also, motion filters allow wide panoramic shots to be slowly panned and scanned. The effect is invaluable when cutting still photos into documentary projects – the motion helps to hold the viewer's attention, and can directly complement commentary by closing in on the people or objects that are being mentioned. Advanced editors such as Vegas [5], MediaStudio Pro [6], Edition and Apple's Final Cut Pro have motion effects tools built in, and they have even been incorporated into Apple's basic editor, iMovie. For those using more basic editors, additional programs, such as Canopus's Imaginate, provide excellent control for adding photos to video projects.

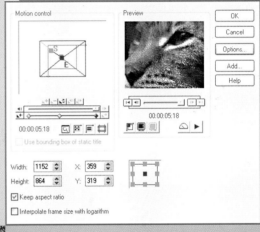

distortion

Advanced editors at the prosumer level allow images to be squeezed and squashed. Pinnacle's Edition and Apple's Final Cut Pro have very tactile hands-on tools for resizing and rescaling images. In Premiere, the Motion Settings editor allows the corners of a video frame to be dragged, distorting the image accordingly. This distortion can also be changed over time. Other distortion filters common to advanced editors include 3D effects such as lens distortion simulators and watery ripple effects.

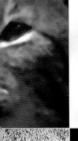

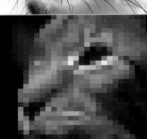

1/ The original, unfiltered image.

2/ Filters that simulate the effect of old, scratched-up film are popular.

3/ Video filters can be used for subtle mood setting or to create extravagant and crazy effects.

4/ Video effects being applied in Sonic Foundry's Vegas.

5/ 6/ Motion blur effects being applied in Vegas and MediaStudio Pro.

picture-in-picture effects

Picture-in-picture effects are seldom used in drama or documentary, but are often seen in magazine programmes on TV, in promotional corporate videos or sales media. The effect is to have one image inset into another, and is often used to show two events occurring simultaneously – such as a puppet and puppeteer or a racing car and driver.

simple effects

The first illustration shows a simple picture-in-picture effect created with Adobe Premiere's 'Zoom' transition. Opening up transition settings in the source monitor, zoom levels for the beginning and end of the effect are set to the same levels, meaning that the superimposed image remains the same size throughout. It can also be repositioned within the small thumbnail frame if need be. This approach is useful if the inset image is to eventually replace the background.

motion effects

This second image shows Premiere's Motion editor – also accessed through the Source monitor – which allows the overlaid clip to be moved over time. Beginning and end points are defined numerically, or by placing thumbnails within a frame. Scale, rotation and transparency may also be set. All parameters can be changed at specific points by adding 'keyframes' to the effect's timeline.

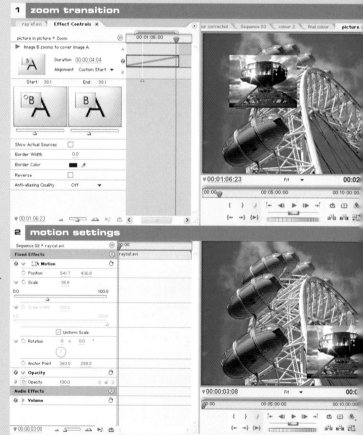

creating effects

Picture-in-picture effects can also be created in some entry-level programs. Here we see the same effect being created in Ulead's VideoStudio 6 [3] and Roxio's VideoWave 5 [4]. In both cases, the inset clip is added using an 'Overlay' effect, and then positioned and resized as required.

1/ Premiere's 'Zoom' transition.
2/ Motion editor in Premiere.
3/ Overlay effects in Ulead's VideoStudio.
4/ A similar effect in Roxio's VideoWave.

3 VideoStudio overlay effect

Picture-in-picture Some beginners' editing programs are rich in effects but their core editing tools are poor. If you're using Roxio's VideoWave or Ulead's VideoStudio, a picture-in-picture effect can be used to perform insert edits (which would otherwise be impossible). With both programs, this is achieved by creating a simple picture-in-picture effect, but setting the scale of the inserted clip to 100%, thereby completely covering the background image.

4 VideoWave overlay effect

titles

Titles are among the most commonly used effects in digital video. Even if you have no need for colour correction, transitions or video filters, it is very likely that you will want to give your movie an on-screen title at the beginning, and tell the viewers who made it at the end.

basic titles

Short title sequences often take the form of static frames with only a few lines of text on each. These are the easiest style of title for audiences to follow, as they don't whizz across the screen or need a magnifying glass to read. Titling tools are provided as part of your video-editing software, and you will be able to use almost any font that is installed on the system. There will also be a choice of text size and colour. Positioning titles on the screen is important – the main title at the beginning of a movie might be centred in the frame, while subtitles for foreign-language sequences would be placed along the bottom. Allow titles to stay on screen long enough to be read, but not so long as to get boring. A few seconds is normally ample for small titles. Use simple fade or cross-dissolve transitions to fade them in and out.

scroll and crawl

Long titles can be tedious if they're presented as hundreds of static frames. If you have a lot of people to credit, present your titles as a big list and run them across the screen. The traditional approach for a movie's end titles is a scrolling motion, in which the list rolls up the screen. However, some situations require a crawl instead, where text moves horizontally across the screen normally from right to left. An example of crawling titles is the breaking news bar on many 24-hour news channels. Be careful with the speed of moving titles. If they go too fast, nobody will be able to read them, while slow titles are painfully boring.

shadows and borders

A drop shadow helps create a sense of separation between titles and their background. Very often a subtle, almost transparent, shadow is all that is needed to lift the text. Experiment with different shadow sizes and transparencies to emphasise the text without drawing attention to the shadow itself. A more obvious method of defining the shape of text in a video frame is to add a coloured border. Borders are far from subtle and should be used for making a bold, brash statement.

transparency

Titles aren't always set against a plain black background. Your video-editing software will also allow text to be superimposed over video. Background transparency is set automatically, and the process is a very easy one. In this case, a little more care must be taken in positioning titles, so as not to obscure important parts of the video image. Choice of text colour is important too – for example, white text on a very bright, pale scene is difficult to read.

other effects

Emboss and bevel effects apply a three-dimensional feel to text by adding new shadows and highlights. Preset options normally include a hard, chiselled stone effect and a soft, rounded plastic appearance. Many editors also allow you to add a metallic or reflective effect for the titles surface. Coloured geometric shapes can also be useful to separate titles from the background completely.

1/ MediaStudio Pro provides a separate title designer – CG Infinity.

2/ Pinnacle applications, such as Studio and Edition, provide a well-integrated title designer called TitleDeko.

3/ Programs such as Premiere have their own titlers, which are capable of some striking results.

4/ A variety of title effects, using different fonts, borders and textures.

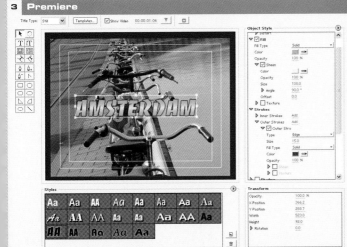

3 Premiere

! *Title safe areas* The extreme edges of your movie won't be visible on normal TV sets. Make sure that your editing program shows a title safe area so you know where your text will be seen, and where it will be hidden. Never allow titles to reach the far left or right of the frame.

! Lighting continuity When trying to seamlessly superimpose one image or video on another, take care to ensure that both share the same kind of lighting arrangement. For example, an actor shot in bright sunlight would not look right superimposed against a dark subterranean background.

working with stills: transparency

Adding photos and graphics to video is a useful technique for illustrating documentaries and creating impressive montages and title sequences. As with titles, images can be picked out from their backgrounds and superimposed on video, or areas of your image can be made transparent, allowing video to show through.

channels

Digital images are composed of different channels, each corresponding to a specific colour. In many cases, there are three main channels (red, green and blue), but graphics intended for print media often use four: cyan, magenta, yellow, and black. Images for video projects should be prepared in the RGB colour space.

Examining channels individually, using a program such as Adobe Photoshop [1], we see that each one is essentially a greyscale image, indicating the intensity of its corresponding colour within the overall picture. White areas are free of colour, while in the black areas it is dense and opaque. The combination of all three channels together produces a seamless full-colour picture.

Image files can contain far more than the basic colour and tone channels. Some image file formats, including PSD, PICT and TIFF files, support up to 24 channels. These non-visible channels, which are called alpha channels, can be used to define areas of transparency within the picture. As with the colour channels, an alpha channel is a simple greyscale image, in which black areas denote complete transparency; white areas keep the image opaque; and midtones indicate varying levels of transparency to provide a blending effect.

In Photoshop (and in many other image editors), you can

1 Photoshop channels

Watermarks Simple graphics with alpha transparency layers are often used to apply logos or watermarks to video; these are now very common on TV channels. Watermarks are used in broadcast to prevent rivals using their footage without crediting or paying them, but can be annoying for the viewer.

overlay and keying

Many DV editing programs automatically detect alpha channels in image files, and set the transparency accordingly. Others may need to be told what kind of key is being used. Keying tells the editor how transparency is applied. So far, we've been denoting transparent and translucent areas with an alpha channel, but there are other ways to create a transparency in stills and video.

Chroma key and Luminance key are techniques used to set transparency in images that don't support dedicated alpha channels. They are particularly useful in imposing one video image on another. Chroma keying identifies a specific colour as the transparent area [3]. This is extremely common in televised weather reports where a blue or green background (chosen because there is no blue or green in human skin tones) is replaced with a map or chart. The technique is also used in movies, to place actors in dangerous or impossible environments.

Luminance keying uses the tonal quality of the image to set transparency, with dark areas

being most transparent, and white areas being opaque. This is rarely the best method of setting solid objects in solid environments, but the effect can be an interesting one.

Advanced editing programs give good control over the level and degree of transparency, and allow users to feather or blend edges of superimposed images, making the effect slightly softer and more natural. Keys can also be reversed if need be, making transparent areas opaque and solid areas transparent.

draw directly on an alpha channel to create a transparent area [2]. Otherwise, graphics and shapes may be incorporated. In the same manner, black-and-white gradients can be used to define the shape and direction of wipes, as we saw with video transitions.

1/ Still images are composed of three or four visible channels and up to 20 more 'alpha' channels.

2/ Here, the transparent area was defined in the main image's alpha channel.

3/ 4/ Chroma key allows areas of colour to be seen as transparent, allowing other images to show through.

! *Layered images* **Some editing programs, such as Apple's Final Cut Express, Final Cut Pro and Adobe's Premiere Pro, allow layered PSD image files to be separated into their component layers, and have each manipulated individually. This is a great tool for creating a sense of depth in composited landscapes or cityscapes.**

working with stills: rostrum effects

Before computers dominated video editing, still photographs and graphics were prepared for movies using rostrum cameras. The set-up would consist of a fixed, mounted camera, trained on a well-lit board, onto which the desired artwork would be placed. The camera could be made to zoom in and out of the image, or to pan and scan from detail to detail. The technique is an important one in documentaries, where you may need to use old photography or documents to complement commentary or other spoken accounts. Today, the effect is produced quickly and easily in good video-editing programs.

1/ Start with as large an image as possible, providing room to crop in.

2/ iMovie's Ken Burns effect.

3/ Motion effects in Vegas, giving independent control over the image, shadow and border effects.

think big

When working with still images, it's very likely that you will want to zoom in on details [1]. Remember that images will remain sharp if you reduce them in size, but if you zoom in too far, you'll just soften the image as its individual pixels are magnified – an effect very similar to that of a camcorder's digital zoom. To give the most versatility, start with the highest resolution image possible. The more pixels that make up an image, the further in you can zoom.

1 large image, max crop

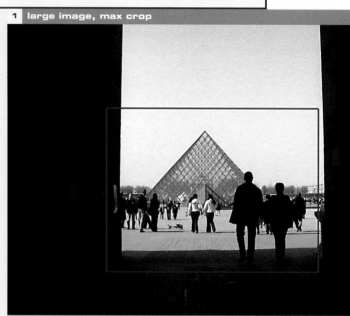

zoom, pan and scan

When using motion filters to emulate a rostrum camera, there are two basic moves that apply: zoom, and pan and scan. As the name suggests, a zoom closes in on a small detail of the image, isolating details such as a face in a crowd. Pan and scan is a process whereby we're already zoomed in on a picture, and moving the camera from one detail to another. It is also a technique that is used extensively in cropping widescreen movies for TV sets without losing too much important action at the edges of the frame.

Slowly does it While you don't want to bore your audience with slow-moving video, it's also important not to dizzy them with lots of fast-moving zooms and pans. Try to set a leisurely pace for motion paths – the movement itself should hold your viewer's attention if the actual image and context are interesting enough.

3 motion control in Vegas

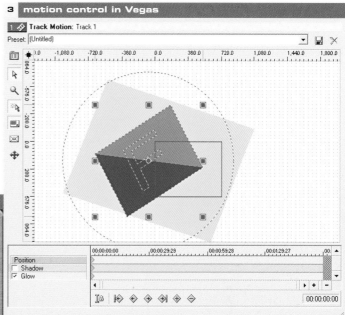

2 motion control in iMovie

in iMovie

iMovie's motion filter for still images is called the Ken Burns effect [2], and is accessed by opening the program's Photos' pane. From here, you'll have access to any library or album that you've compiled in Apple's basic photo-editing tool, iPhoto. The Ken Burns effect is a simple linear movement, which can contain a directional motion and zoom. Two sliders are provided: one sets the duration of the effect, and the other specifies the extent of the zoom. Clicking and dragging the preview image, as well as adjusting the zoom, allows you to set start and end points for the motion. Once done, clicking Apply drops the image onto the timeline as a video clip.

in Vegas

Sonic's Vegas, like many other editing programs, allows images to be manipulated as a frame within a frame [3]. The picture can be resized and repositioned in relation to a secondary frame that represents the viewer's TV screen. Images can have shadow or glow applied to make them stand out from the background, and they can be rotated too. Unlike iMovie, Vegas's effects palette includes a small timeline on which keyframes can be set denoting controlled stages of the image's motion. This allows a complex progression of motion effects to be applied to the image rather than relying on one single action.

POSE   MATERIAL   FACE   HAIR   CL

Light Controls.   Editing Tools.

runner 1.pz3

▼ Move X and Z.

▼ Document Display Style.

Frame 5   ▼ Main Camera

Frame: 001 of 030

Loop

special effects

When you think of special effects, you are more likely to picture spaceships and explosions than colour correction filters and gradient wipes. And despite what you might think, the more exciting side of special effects isn't restricted to professional features with a big budget. There is a lot you can do quite cheaply on your home computer if you have the talent and vision for it!

animation

Computer-generated 3D animation is now the mainstay of science fiction and fantasy cinema. While early efforts in computer-generated imagery were restricted to mechanical and geometric forms such as spaceships, the technology has progressed to the point where movie-makers are creating computer-generated monsters and fantasy characters to share the screen with real actors. Well-featured modelling and animation programs such as Lightwave are expensive, and require some genuine talent in sculpture and design, but the results they yield are often breathtaking. For the beginner, programs such as Ulead's Cool 3D provide a good introduction to 3D. The program serves as an excellent 3D title generator, and also allows simple models to be created from a combination of geometric shapes. They can be animated too. Also worth a look is Curious Labs' Poser [1]. This enables 3D modelling and

animation of human and animal forms. The quality of its rendered images and video is superb, and there is a massive online community of users, sharing and selling new models and animation scripts. Bryce is another popular program, this time for landscape modelling. It integrates well with models created in Poser.

video paint

Video paint (also known as rotoscoping) is the process of drawing on video frames. There is a good range of programs available at different price points, all designed for different purposes. In this case [2], I used a very inexpensive program called AlamDV to add a lightsabre effect to the animated movie created in Poser. The program is timeline based, and allows the light effect to be rotated and rescaled from

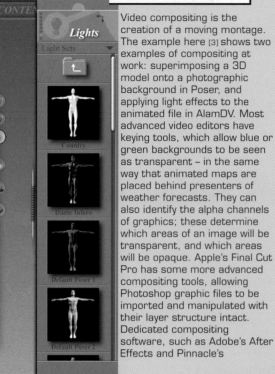

compositing

Video compositing is the creation of a moving montage. The example here [3] shows two examples of compositing at work: superimposing a 3D model onto a photographic background in Poser, and applying light effects to the animated file in AlamDV. Most advanced video editors have keying tools, which allow blue or green backgrounds to be seen as transparent – in the same way that animated maps are placed behind presenters of weather forecasts. They can also identify the alpha channels of graphics; these determine which areas of an image will be transparent, and which areas will be opaque. Apple's Final Cut Pro has some more advanced compositing tools, allowing Photoshop graphic files to be imported and manipulated with their layer structure intact. Dedicated compositing software, such as Adobe's After Effects and Pinnacle's

3

Commotion, takes things further still, enabling a seamless integration of video clips and graphics. This software provides extensive control over transparency and movement of individual elements in layers. Compositing is often a complex and time-consuming business, but for title sequences and animations, the results can be well worth it.

1/ Programs such as Poser provide a good way in to the world of 3D modelling and animation.

2/ AlamDV is an effective and very affordable video paint and special effects program.

3/ The finished composite.

one frame to the next. AlamDV is hugely popular with budding action movie-makers, being ideal for muzzle flash effects in gunfight sequences and all kinds of light effects for sci-fi. Another video paint program, simply called Video Paint, is supplied as part of Ulead's prosumer editing suite, MediaStudio Pro. It is nicely featured and has some decent compositing tools too.

2 video painting in AlamDV

4 share

When desktop video production first began to hit the mainstream, most people didn't think much further than copying finished projects to VHS tape. In recent years, recordable DVD has become affordable, and widespread uptake of broadband internet connections makes streaming video a viable option for reaching large audiences without the need to make physical copies of your work.

These new publishing options bring with them increased levels of interactivity, adding new dimensions to movies such as the ability to skip between scenes or conjure up subtitles as and when they are needed. With the right software, you can

sharing movies

also make DVD projects with additional audio tracks for commentaries or foreign-language translations, and live events can be presented with multiple video angles, allowing viewers to flip from one camera to another. It is also relatively easy to integrate video into PowerPoint presentations or multimedia CD-ROMs. Video can even be sent and received by mobile phones.

The potential of these tapeless video formats is as great for the casual home user as for corporate marketeers and big businesses. We're all keen to communicate in the most dynamic way possible!

1

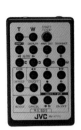

back to tape

Regardless of what format you eventually choose to share your movie, tape is still important for archiving work. Making a DV copy of finished work is essential, but there is still much need for VHS tapes too.

output to DV

A DV tape is probably the highest quality back-up you can make of your movie. Digital output to tape uses the same FireWire port as capture. And just as video capture is technically lossless, the same goes for output. Providing there are no flaws in the tape itself, the video you record back to DV should be identical to the movie on your hard drive.

As with capture, editing software can control the playback and recording commands of the attached camcorder or digital VCR, and all good DV editing software will be able to output your edited movie straight from the timeline with no additional processing. Unfortunately, a very small handful of entry-level programs still require edited movies to be saved to the hard drive as self-contained DV video files before they can be sent back out to tape.

Make sure that your camcorder can receive a DV signal via FireWire. In the EU, most camcorders have had their DV inputs disabled in an attempt to avoid excessive taxation on import. There was a time when enthusiasts who had been stung by these restrictions could re-enable DV-input using a small hardware device or a simple computer program, but the creators of these solutions have been forced to cease trading under threat of legal action. Sadly, this means that if you've already invested in a 'nEUtered' camcorder, your only option for making full-quality DV back-ups may be to spend more money on a second camcorder or a DV deck.

2

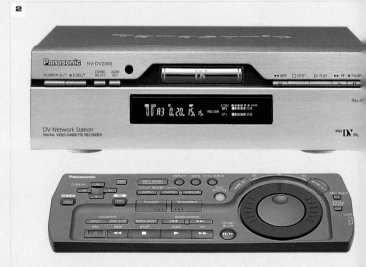

Video standards Regardless of whether you are sending your movie to tape or DVD, it is important to check the video standard of the person receiving it. The UK, most of mainland Europe, Australia and New Zealand use a TV system called PAL, which has a different image size, frame rate and colour sampling to NTSC, a standard used in the USA, Canada and Japan. France has another standard called SECAM, while some Middle Eastern and African nations use a derivative called MESECAM. If you are sending movies abroad, make sure that the recipient will be able to watch them. Standard conversion VCRs are available at a price, to create VHS copies in the standard you require, and there are software options too for digital files – at least for converting between PAL and NTSC.

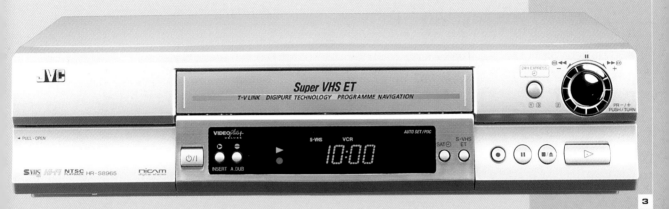

3

output to VHS

VHS is not defunct yet. And even though DVD provides better quality, and streaming media is more exciting, there's no escaping the fact that almost everybody owns a VHS video recorder. You can be almost certain that the recipient has the wherewithal to watch a VHS tape, while CD-ROMs depend on having the right kind of computer for playback, and even DVD players might have trouble with certain types of recordable CD and DVD media. The newer formats may be exciting, but they are still prone to teething troubles. VHS,

on the other hand, is a safe bet – albeit dull and conservative.

Also worth remembering is that VHS copies are easy to make – feed video into your home VCR, insert a tape and press record. It's great for making quick viewing copies of work in progress, without having to go to the lengths of media encoding or disc authoring. If you are using real-time hardware on your system, you'll be able to output an analogue AV signal straight from the timeline for recording to VHS tape. If not, it's likely that the

editing system provides only a DV output via FireWire. If this is the case, you'll find that most DV-in enabled camcorders and all DV VCRs are able to output an analogue video signal via composite and S-video channels while receiving DV via FireWire – use it as a signal converter. If you're one of the unlucky souls with a 'nEUtered' DV camcorder, signal converter boxes are available to do the same job – turning DV output into an analogue stream.

1/ Many DV camcorders accept an incoming DV signal via FireWire – but make sure you check before buying if you live in the EU.

2/ A MiniDV recorder is a good investment if you do a lot of editing. It can remain permanently connected to your system and monitor.

3/ There's still no escaping the need to make VHS copies of movies, and a good recorder is a wise purchase. SVHS machines provide S-video inputs that are useful for making good VHS copies as well as SVHS recordings.

1
O RECORDER   DMR-E100H

DVD-RAM/DVD-R

HDD & DVD
RECORDING

EJECT

PC CARD

DVD
VIDEO
RAM

RESSIVE SCAN

REC DVD-RAM   SP
PLAY   PG
7   0:03:52

burn to disc: DVD

Recordable DVD hit the mainstream IT market in 2000, and its uptake has been phenomenal among video and computing enthusiasts. DVD video production is now an easy and cost-effective means of delivering high-quality interactive video, and there are some excellent disc-authoring tools available for beginners as well as professionals. As with all new media developments, nothing is as straightforward as it should be, however. There are some serious limitations and pitfalls to be aware of.

video and audio formats

DVD uses a form of video compression called MPEG-2. It has the same picture resolution and frame rate as DV, but is far more compressed. While each frame of DV video is a single, self-contained image, MPEG-2 video compression examines the differences between frames and only updates areas that have changed. The result is a generally high-quality video with a much smaller file size. Most DVD authoring programs allow you to use MPEG streams that contain audio and video together (these are known as program streams), while others insist on elementary streams in which video and audio are saved as separate files.

Audio formats supported by the DVD video standard include linear PCM audio (the same type of sound format used by DV), or compressed DTS and Dolby AC-3 formats. The latter options can be stereo or surround-sound, depending on how adventurous you are with your movie, but the encoders are often expensive, due to the format's hefty licensing charges. MPEG audio (which is often created in program streams) delivers good quality and is easy to produce, but is only a recognised part of the PAL DVD specification for playback in Europe, Australia and New Zealand. Many NTSC DVD players in the US and Canada provide mute playback if the disc carries MPEG audio.

DVD formats

The first recordable DVD format to appear was Panasonic's rewritable DVD-RAM standard. The discs provide good reliable data back-up, but they are normally enclosed in a plastic cartridge and – even when removed – aren't recognised by set-top players as DVD discs.

Things became interesting with the first appearance of Pioneer's DVD-R format, but prices of recorders and discs were kept artificially high out of fear within the movie industry that home users would use it to make pirate copies of borrowed or rented movies. The first mainstream recordable DVD format appeared in 2000, with General-Use DVD-R and DVD-RW, which were (supposedly) unable to be used for movie piracy. Sadly, they were also unable to be recognised by a lot of the DVD players that had already been installed in people's homes. Hot on the heels of DVD-R came Philips' DVD+R and DVD+RW formats. These are very similar to Pioneer's standards, but their playability on set-top DVD players is slightly different to that of DVD-R. At the time of writing, these two formats are still battling it out to become the single recordable DVD standard. In the meantime, the message to movie-makers (particularly those making corporate and wedding videos) is clear – you'll need both!

DVD recorders

1/ Set-top DVD recorders provide an easy way to copy video to disc, but provide limited tools for customising menus and overall presentation.

2/ DVD burners provide the most versatility for DVD video creation, providing you have good authoring software.

3/ Not all shiny recordable discs are the same! There are two competing DVD standards to watch out for: DVD-R/RW and DVD+R/RW.

4/ A good selection of high-quality, inexpensive MPEG encoders are available on the internet.

Set-top DVD recorders do pretty much the same job as a VHS VCR, allowing TV programs to be recorded and videos to be copied – but these recordings are made to disc in a way that should be playable on an ordinary DVD player. For the most part, recordings made by these machines are good, with many even offering a FireWire input for connection to DV camcorders. But recording features can vary depending on the machine and video format you are using. At present, the most user-friendly recordings I've seen have been made to DVD+R and DVD+RW disc, providing basic menus and chapter selection features for navigating the recorded videos. They can also be played in ordinary DVD players (providing those players are able to recognise the disc type).

But while set-top recorders provide a quick and easy way of copying your work to disc, they don't allow menus to be customised with your own designs, and provide little control over menu structure. For that, you'll need to author your project on a computer.

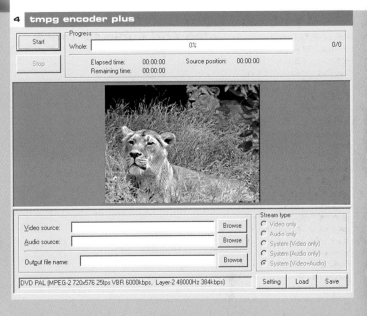

DVD burners

DVD burners are computer drives that write to DVD discs and also act as a DVD-ROM drive. Most will burn to CD-R and CD-RW too, and in only a few short years, their prices have fallen to a point where they're pushing CD burners out of the market. The first mainstream DVD burners to appear were restricted to a single recordable DVD standard – be it Pioneer's DVD-R/RW or Philips DVD+R/RW – but many companies (including Pioneer) now support both standards with their latest generation of drives. This means that movie-makers can provide discs to clients with more confidence that they will play on their DVD players.

> **! Keep menus short** If you are making DVDs with motion menus (menus that use video for backgrounds and buttons rather than still images), keep them short. The longer you make an animated menu, the more space it will take on the DVD disc. Ideally, a motion menu should be kept to

30 seconds or less, and, with any luck, your viewer will have chosen a movie or slideshow within that time. If it hasn't, the menu will just keep looping until it does. If the menu has accompanying music, try to pick something that won't drive people mad if the menu is left to loop for a few minutes.

> **! Keep it organised** Remember that menus can link to more menus – you don't need to cram all your options on one screen. For example, don't put the button for a movie on the same menu screen as the individual chapter stops. Instead, create a root menu with a link to the movie and another link to a sub-menu offering a choice of chapters. This is something that iDVD wisely does by default.

burn to disc: DVD authoring

Regardless of whether you are a video novice or a keen enthusiast, there is a good selection of software available to help you create impressive DVD video presentations. The most advanced features, such as multiple video angles, multiple audio tracks and subtitles, are reserved for the prosumer and professional programs, but even inexpensive beginners' software should provide all you need to create discs with strong design, chapter markers and scene-selection menus.

chapter marker

A chapter marker is an index point on your video, normally denoting the beginning of a new scene, and allowing viewers to skip from one scene to another using the player's remote control. Markers can also be linked directly to menu buttons to create scene-selection menus.

Apple iDVD

Chapter marking is possible for iDVD projects, but it's all done in Apple's entry-level editing program, iMovie [1]. Don't worry if your video hasn't been edited in iMovie – just make a DV copy to the hard drive, and import it into iMovie's timeline. Click the DVD button located below the program's clip pane. Now place the playhead on the frame where you want to set a new chapter marker, and click the Add Chapter button. A thumbnail image representing the marker will appear in the clip pane. When all markers have been placed, click Create iDVD project to send the movie to iDVD.

Pinnacle's Studio

DVD authoring is done in Studio's main editing interface [2]. Before you can start marking chapters, a menu must be added to the project. There's no need to design anything yet, but

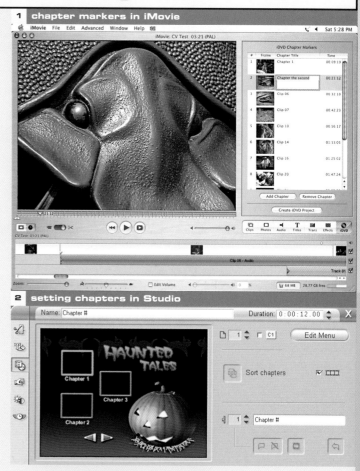

1 chapter markers in iMovie

2 setting chapters in Studio

once it's there on the timeline, you can play or scrub through your movie, and click a Chapter Flag button in Studio's DVD editor toolbox. Alternatively,

right-click at the top of the timeline and select Set Disc Chapter. These chapter markers will automatically be linked to the menu you created.

Ulead's DVD Workshop

Import a movie into DVD Workshop and add it to your project. Double-clicking on its thumbnail icon opens it in a video viewer, allowing you to play the video, scrub through it on a timeline or advance one frame at a time. Chapter markers are set by clicking an Insert Chapter button [3]. Each new chapter point is represented by a thumbnail icon in the chapter list that runs down the right-hand side of the screen. These can be used to create links in scene-selection menus at a later stage.

4 slideshows in iDVD

1/ Chapter points for Apple's iDVD are set up on iMovie's timeline.

2/ Pinnacle's Studio provides a control panel for applying and customising chapter points. It also allows them to be applied directly to the timeline.

3/ DVD Workshop's interface showing a main video monitor and a list of chapter points running down the right-hand side. New chapter points are made by clicking the Insert Chapter button at the far right of the playback controls.

4/ Even simple programs such as iDVD allow slideshows to be added to DVD presentations as well as video.

5/ Menus give access to individual movies, slideshows and chapters.

6/ Programs such as Pinnacle's Studio provide excellent menu design tools.

3 setting chapters in DVD Workshop

slideshows

DVDs don't just have to contain movies and menus – you can also add slideshows created from a sequence of still images. All good authoring programs allow this [4]. You can specify how long each picture appears on screen and, in some cases, add forward and back buttons, allowing viewers to flick through the photos in their own time.

menus

Menus are navigational screens that provide access to movies, their individual chapters, or slideshows [5]. Authoring programs at the entry level provide ready-made design templates for menus, in which all buttons and layouts are automatically generated. While you can often choose your own background image and enter your own text, the most basic programs don't provide much layout control. Fortunately, things are changing, and programs such as iDVD, Studio 8 [6] and DVD Workshop have excellent menu design tools. Note too, that the images used in menus don't necessarily have to be static images. Try using a video clip as the background rather than a photo. If you're using thumbnail icons as buttons to access movies, these can often be animated too.

5 menu screen in iDVD

6 menu design tools in Studio

1

Disc compatibility Even if a DVD player is able to play VCD and SVCD discs, it still might not be able to play the ones that you make. Many players are simply incapable of recognising recordable CDs. It has nothing to do with the video encoding or the way it's burned, just simply that the disc itself can't be read. Some players are better than others, and some discs are better than others. In my own tests, I found that rewritable CD-RW media was often better at playing in stubborn machines than write-once CD-R discs. If you are buying a player with the intention of playing home-made discs, I would recommend taking some of those discs with you to the showroom and asking to try them out on the display models.

burn to disc: VCD and SVCD

Before DVD recording became a possibility for home movie-makers, many of us turned to VideoCD and its higher quality successor, Super VideoCD in a bid to publish video on little shiny discs.

the formats

VideoCD (VCD) is a hugely popular video format in the Far East. Before the appearance of DVD, VCD was as popular in the East as VHS was in the West. The format is compact and allows instant access to scenes in the same way that DVD does. Players are inexpensive too, as many components are common to audio CD players. Commercially released VCDs are pressed in the same factories as audio CDs too, helping keep replication costs down. On the downside, VCD's picture quality isn't significantly better than that of VHS, and a single disc can hold only around 70 minutes of footage, meaning that feature films have to be split across two CDs.

VCD uses MPEG-1 video and audio compression – similar to the MPEG-2 streams used in DVD, but with a much smaller frame size and lower data rate. Encoding for VCD production must be done to very strict parameters, allowing no margin for error at all. Thankfully, most good MPEG encoders provide a ready-made VCD encoding template.

Super VideoCD (SVCD) was introduced in 1998, partly in an attempt to avoid licensing costs associated with DVD. Like DVD, SVCD uses MPEG-2 video compression, but with a lower data rate and a slightly smaller frame size – squashing the picture's width to 480 pixels rather than the full DVD resolution of 720. Because of the higher quality video, a single SVCD disc can hold only around 40 minutes of footage. The format never took off to any huge extent, but SVCD-compatible encoding templates are provided with most MPEG encoders.

authoring

While Apple's DVD authoring software only supports the DVD format, most Windows-based programs at the entry-level offer you the choice of publishing movies as DVD, VCD or SVCD discs. DVD is the better choice with regard to quality, but if you have yet to invest in a DVD burner, VCD and SVCD represent decent alternatives for creating CD-based presentations.

As with DVD, VCD and SVCD formats support menus, chapter markers and slideshows as well as the movies themselves, but interactive highlighting of buttons isn't possible on menus. Instead, each button is given a number, corresponding to numerical buttons on the player's remote control.

Client compatibility Makers of wedding videos and corporate presentations are often asked to deliver work on disc, be it **DVD**, **VCD** or **SVCD**. Make sure that the clients' players can read your discs before you agree to take their money. Many freelance professionals have taken to giving their clients new **DVD** players along with the finished movies, just to make sure they aren't stuck with discs they can't watch.

1/ It's still possible to find CD players with the ability to play VideoCDs if you look around.

2/ 3/ These preview screens from Ulead MovieFactory show how VCD and DVD menus differ. VCD and SVCD titles don't allow viewers to highlight and click hotspots on the menu. Instead, options are chosen using numerical buttons on the remote control.

playback

Because of its immense popularity in the Far East, almost all set-top DVD players are able to play VCD discs too. Be aware though, that there have been two versions of VCD over the years. While VCD was originally launched in 1993, support for interactive menus wasn't added until 1995. While most DVD players recognise and play VCD discs, some are only compatible with the original VCD 1.1 standard rather than the later VCD 2.0 discs. Fortunately, video on the newer discs will play – you just won't get access to the menus.

SVCD has had a hard battle against the popularity of DVD, and its uptake hasn't come anywhere near that of VCD. Because of this, the format is supported by far fewer set-top DVD players. An inexpensive player from China is far more likely to play SVCD discs than a big-brand model from Japan.

Of course, VCD and SVCD playback isn't limited to playback on set-top DVD players – they can be read on any computer with a CD-ROM drive, providing you have suitable player software. A quick search on the net will uncover a good selection of inexpensive shareware applications for download.

! *Metadata* Metadata is
information added to video files
that doesn't affect video or audio
content. Metadata might take the
form of commands for event
streaming, but the most common
use is to provide title, artist and
copyright information for display
in the viewer's player software.

share on the web

There are two ways to deliver video on the internet: providing video for download, and streaming video. Downloads are copied from the internet to the viewer's computer hard drive and played back from there. Streaming video is played directly from the internet and is never actually stored on the viewer's system. Delivering video on the web can make movies available all over the world with no need to make physical copies. It is an exciting and immediate form of media delivery, but the technology is still developing and there are many limitations and drawbacks.

speed

Even with the widespread uptake of broadband internet services, video files still need to be very heavily compressed in order to stream over standard DSL connections. This often means having to settle for small image sizes, reduced frame rates, and mono sound. There is also some confusion to overcome in the choice of streaming video file formats available – and the need to decide what kind of media player software your target audience is most likely to have installed.

2 Windows Media Player

formats

The choice of streaming video formats can be a little daunting – and it's unlikely that you will want to use them all. On the plus side, however, competition in streaming video is now so fierce that quality of video compression techniques is improving in leaps and bounds.

RealVideo

Real Networks was one of the pioneers of streaming media on the internet, and is still at the forefront, competing fiercely with Microsoft's Windows Media Format. RealVideo gives good picture and sound quality (considering the low bandwidth used), but viewers must have the company's media player, called RealPlayer, installed on their systems. The basic RealPlayer is free, but users are strongly encouraged by Real Networks to

spend money to upgrade to a bigger, better Plus version. Many IT, video and internet enthusiasts have a great dislike for Real Networks software, as well as the company's attitude towards advertising and marketing. There is a good selection of encoding tools available for making RealVideo files for the web, but most are for Windows only. At the time of writing, RealVideo encoding software (particularly for the latest version of the format) is virtually non-existent on the Mac.

QuickTime

QuickTime is Apple's video format. Like AVI files used in Windows systems, QuickTime files can use a vast number of compression methods to squash files for delivery. A QuickTime file might be streaming video for the web or a full quality DV file freshly captured from a camcorder, but they are all viewed in the same player. As with RealPlayer, Apple's

QuickTime Player is available as a basic free player as well as a chargeable program called QuickTime Pro. But unlike RealPlayer Plus, QuickTime Pro provides good tools for media encoding too. Playback and encoding tools are available for Mac and Windows PCs, but the overall uptake of QuickTime Player is rather limited compared

to the number of RealPlayer and Windows Media Player programs in use. What's more, many enthusiasts feel that QuickTime's streaming performance isn't as fluid as that of rival formats. However, it makes an ideal standard for providing material to download and view offline.

1/ 2/ 3/ RealVideo, Windows Media and QuickTime are the most commonly used formats for streaming video on the internet.

Windows Media

As far as picture and sound quality goes, Windows Media sits at the top of the game, alongside RealVideo, and is slowly pulling away, leaving the competition behind. One of the most exciting recent developments for the format is surround-sound audio tracks for broadband video files. Windows Media plays back in Windows Media Player, which is a standard part of the Windows Operating system, free to update and also free to download for Mac users. However, while Windows Media can be viewed on almost any type of system, the latest encoding tools for making files are currently available only for Windows systems – leaving Mac-based movie-makers high and dry.

3 QuickTime

Blocko tape 1a_CD.mov

00:01:41

4/ 5/ Creating a web page with embedded video is easy in VideoStudio, but the results are very basic.

6/ Adobe GoLive offers direct support for RealVideo and QuickTime.

7/ Setting size can be a hassle, as dimensions must also accommodate the control bar, but video pages can be customised however you want.

8/ Many video sites feature well-designed players with customised controls – but they have all been carefully hand coded.

streaming servers

For small audiences, video can be streamed from a standard web server – the same server that hosts your HTML pages and pictures. This doesn't provide any protection for your movie, however, and it would be very easy for anyone to download it to their hard drives. Web servers normally offer a very limited amount of data transfer every month, and if your movie is popular, you'll find that you have exceeded your quota very quickly. What is more, most ordinary web servers aren't capable of sustaining the large amounts of data transfer that is required to serve video to tens or sometimes hundreds of people at once.

If you plan to be popular, you will need to have your movie stored on a dedicated streaming media server. These servers are designed to meet high demands for data and sustain transfer for prolonged periods. Streaming servers also help prevent video files from being downloaded to the viewer's computer, and provide detailed information about which movies have been watched, how much of them were watched, and what media player software was used. They're not cheap though – and the more people watch your movie, the more expensive they become.

Data rates Even though broadband internet is exciting and opens up all sorts of possibilities for media delivery, remember that there are still many people connecting to the net with basic dial-up modems. You must provide a narrowband version of your movie if you want to reach the widest possible audience. Thankfully, Windows Media and RealVideo allow several versions of the video (each with a different data rate) to be packaged into a single file. This allows you to create only one web page to cover all connection speeds, and it also means that the viewer's player can drop to a lighter stream if online traffic becomes too heavy.

adding video

You can link a web page to movie files in exactly the same way that you would link to other web pages or sites. It is the simplest way to provide access to videos, but they all open in software players, rather than being integrated into the design of the page itself. Video players can be embedded into web pages, but this often requires substantial skills in hand coding, as web design programs still provide only a very basic set of tools. If you are stuck using HTML editor software, you'll find yourself adding plug-ins to web pages, then trying to tell the software what kind of media it is embedding into the page.

VideoStudio

Ulead's VideoStudio offers the means to create streaming video files from edited projects and automatically embed them into web pages. First off, encode the movie into the required streaming format – in this case, RealVideo or Windows Media. Then, from the Export menu, choose Web Page, making sure it is saved to the same folder as the movie you created. The resulting page is very basic – just video on a blank background – but can be built upon and redesigned using any HTML editor. The downside is that this new script is dependent on the video being hosted on a standard web server, and it will need to have its coding altered manually if the video is being served from elsewhere.

event streaming

Event streaming brings a rich sense of interactivity to streaming video presentations. Simple commands are encoded into a video stream that cause events to happen within the web page itself. These events can be subtitles, illustrative images, or the opening of whole new web pages. Event streaming is enormously useful for creating online tutorials and educational presentations, but it is held back slightly due to the fact that

Windows Media, QuickTime and RealVideo all support different types of events, and there is only a limited selection common to all three. Also, while event commands can be embedded into files using Premiere (under Windows) or Cleaner (on the Mac), there are few HTML editors designed to work with event streaming pages, making layout control tricky unless you are good at hand coding.

Adobe GoLive

Adobe GoLive's Objects palette has specific plug-in command icons for adding RealVideo or QuickTime files to your web pages. Sadly, there are no such options for other formats such as Windows Media. To add RealVideo or QuickTime, drag and drop the appropriate icon over to your web page. In the Inspector palette, specify which video file is being used (it helps if the movie is already online and you can enter the URL). GoLive can't automatically decide how big the video is, so you will need to enter dimensions too. Be aware that the dimensions you enter will also include the player's control panel, so do some previews, and work

7 GoLive workspace

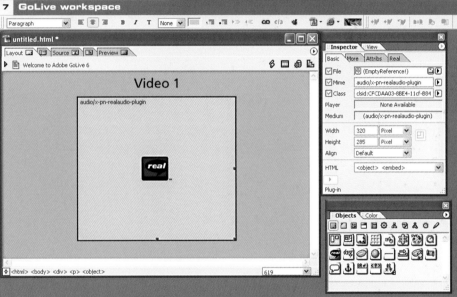

6 GoLive palette

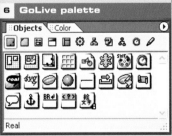

out how big the controller will be. If the controls are 45 pixels high and your movie is 320 x 240 pixels in size, you'll need to set a dimension of 320 x 285.

To add a Windows Media file, drag the basic plug-in icon over to the page. Enter the URL for your video file as we did in the previous example, but in the Inspector's

Mime files, choose either video/msvideo or video/x-msvideo from the drop-down menu. Enter dimensions as before – taking care to allow just the right amount of space for the player controls. If you look closely at the Mime menu, you will see options for other formats such as AVI files and MPEG.

SHOWREEL - VIDEO

WILDLIFE

MUSIC

MAIN MENU

HTML

Web pages can be viewed from CDs just as easily as from internet servers – a lot of programs provide HTML-based help files these days. HTML pages are a safe bet for providing interactive content, as every computer now has a web browser, and you can easily develop a presentation that can be viewed by Macs as well as Windows PCs. Design your presentation the same way you would a website, and burn the whole lot to a CD-R. You may need to include instructions on how to launch the presentation though.

multimedia and CD-ROM

Movies often need to be worked into multimedia presentations or CD-ROM discs. The standard tool for creating interactive, media-rich CD-ROMs is Macromedia Director, but it is extremely expensive, and has a rather steep learning curve that I won't go into here. There are some less expensive options, however.

video formats

Take care when choosing a video format for multimedia, as not all computer systems will have the same range of video codecs as you – there is a danger that you will include videos that your viewer's computer can't open. QuickTime files tend to be safe, but viewers using Windows systems may need to install the QuickTime Player software before viewing the presentation. VCD-compatible MPEG-1 files should also be fine.

Try to keep the data rate low, so that it plays smoothly from a CD-ROM. In the early days of multimedia design, 200Kb/s was considered the limit, but faster CD-ROM drives now allow you to get away with more. On the other hand, video compression quality has improved immensely since then too, so you probably won't need to.

interactivity

Interactivity refers to the element of choice – the ability of the user to decide which media elements they want to see.

PowerPoint

PowerPoint presentations are composed of slides that appear in a prescribed sequence, and can contain graphics, text, audio and video. There's no interactive control over their order, however, and you can't pick and choose which slides to look at. To add video to a PowerPoint presentation, first click on the frame at the point where you want to place a movie. From the Insert menu, choose Movies and Sounds, then select Movie From File. Select the video file you want to insert. Any format supported by Windows Media Player is accepted, and once a movie is selected, PowerPoint will ask whether you want it to begin playing immediately when the frame is loaded, or to wait until viewers click on it. Movie files are easily dragged into any position in the frame, but avoid resizing it, as this could cause a lag or stutter during playback.

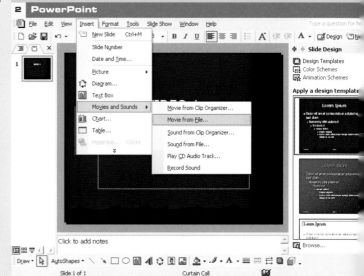

Illuminatus Opus

Digital Workshop's Illuminatus Opus is one of a select handful of programs that provides rich multimedia tools at a fraction of the cost of programs like Director. It is very powerful software, capable of producing first-rate interactive multimedia presentations, from promotional CD-ROMs to educational discs, and even games. It also enables projects to be uploaded to the internet and viewed as websites. On the downside, Opus is only available for Windows PCs, and most of the presentations it creates are limited to playback on Windows systems. An export program called Flex is available to publish presentations into a Flash format that can be read by both systems, but Flash has very poor support for popular video formats.

To add video in Opus: Select Open from the File menu and choose your movie file. The same result can be had by choosing Video from the Insert menu, and drawing a rectangular area on the page where you want the movie to be positioned. You'll then be prompted to choose a movie file, say how many times it will play, and control its size on the screen. Movies can be made mute or invisible when not actually playing. Alternatively, dragging a Video Player onto a page provides a movie with playback controls including play, pause, stop, and the means to skip to the beginning or end of the file.

1/ Multimedia menus provide a graphic interface with links to media or information.

2/ Adding video to PowerPoint presentations is easy, but there's little interactivity on offer.

3/ 4/ Multimedia authoring programs such as Opus provide good levels of interactivity and design control.

5/ A simple Autorun script will allow the disc to launch automatically.

publishing

In Opus and PowerPoint, projects can be packaged as self-running presentations that can then be burned to CD if you have a CD writer and writing software. HTML presentations can be copied directly to CD, so long as all the media files are provided and properly linked in the pages. Opus also creates an autorun.inf file that is included with the CD and instructs the viewer's PC to launch your presentation automatically when the disc is inserted. Some advanced CD writing programs, such as Roxio's WinOnCD, can create autorun files too, allowing you to specify which file is launched when the disc is loaded – be it a PowerPoint presentation or your first HTML page.

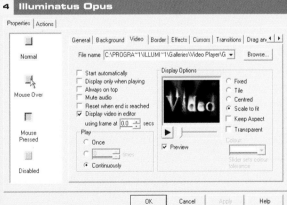

5 Notepad

File Edit Format View Help

```
[autorun]
open="start /m index.htm"
icon=movie.ico
```

direct capture in Studio

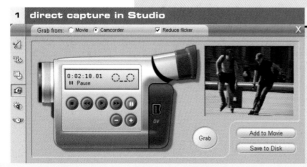

Grab from: ○ Movie ● Camcorder ☑ Reduce flicker   X

0:02:18.01
▐▐ Pause

Grab

Add to Movie

Save to Disk

during capture

Video capture tools of most video-editing programs also support the capture of individual frames as image files. Most will save the frames in their native state, so you'll have to make some corrections in a photo-editing program such as Photoshop. But it's worthwhile hunting through program preferences to see what kind of processing tools are on offer. Where possible, choose adaptive deinterlacing and image resizing. Also, beware that some programs might choose a very low resolution for saving image files. You should be able to correct this in the program's settings.

In most cases, as with Pinnacle's Studio, and Ulead's VideoStudio, a dedicated capture frame button is provided, making still image capture a single-click operation. For many others, especially those at the advanced level, frames can only be grabbed from DV video files that have already been captured to the hard drive.

capturing video frames

If you are putting details of your movie on a website, emailing information to magazines, or even designing a cover for a video or DVD, it's very likely that you will need to isolate frames of your video and use them as digital photos.

! Know your limits Be aware that frames grabbed from DV tape have a very limited resolution, and are not ideal for print. They have also had their detail halved through deinterlacing, and there are obvious limits to how far you can enlarge them before they become soft and pixelated. If you need images for a press pack and promotional materials, your best bet is to take them separately during the shoot using a stills camera.

in camera

Camcorders equipped with a memory card often have the means to copy selected frames from DV tape to card. The resulting files tend to be a little smaller than the original frame, at 640 x 480 pixels, but the process takes care of many correction processes, such as deinterlacing and compensation for pixel shape. The saved images can then be copied directly to the system via a card reader, or by connecting the camera to the system via USB. Panasonic's DV camcorders have a Digital Stills interface, designed specifically for copying video frames to computers as digital image files.

2 iMovie export

Export: To QuickTime

Formats: Expert Settings...

Your movie will be compressed with appropriate settings and may be reduced in width and height as well. This operation may take several minutes to complete.

Cancel   Export

3 iMovie naming

Save As: image.bmp
Where: 📁 Desktop

Export: Movie to BMP   Options...
Use: Millions of Colors

Cancel   Save

4 iMovie compression

Compression Settings

Compressor
BMP
Millions of Colors

Quality
Least Low Medium High Best

Cancel   OK

! Remember where they went! Many video-editing programs don't ask you where still images are to be saved – they just drop them into a default folder along with the video files you're using in your edit. Pay attention, and make a note of where the files go, as you will need to find them yourself when attaching them to emails, working them into websites or opening them in photo-editing programs.

from captured files

Some editors can isolate frames from captured DV files at any stage during playback, but in most cases, frame grabbing is done with the program's export tools. Frames can be saved individually, or as a sequence, allowing you to select the most appropriate image at a later stage. Note that with some Mac-based programs, such as iMovie, Final Cut Pro and Final Cut Express, it is necessary to mark the area of the timeline you want to save as image files, and export via QuickTime. It's likely that you will have a choice of image formats too, and at this stage it's best to choose an uncompressed format such as bitmap files (for Windows systems) or PICT files if you're using a Mac.

As before, a hunt in the program's preferences may uncover settings for deinterlacing and rescaling pixels. Otherwise, these corrections will have to be done elsewhere.

deinterlacing

Each video frame is composed of two interlaced fields. Unless your video editor has separated these fields, objects in the saved image may appear to have jagged edges – there is a slight time difference between the two fields, so any fast-moving objects will appear jaggy when the two fields are condensed into a single image. Fortunately, good photo-editing tools, such as Adobe Photoshop, can deinterlace the image, and this should be done before any other image editing. Photoshop's deinterlacing filter allows you to decide whether to keep odd or even fields, and there can be a

significant difference between the two if there is a lot of fast motion, or if flashing lights were present in the scene. There is also a choice between duplicating the remaining frames or interpolating the image to patch up areas of the picture where unwanted fields have been removed.

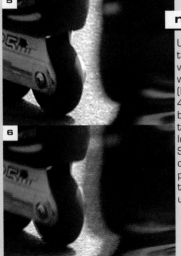

7 Photoshop deinterlacing

1/ Image capture direct from DV tape in Pinnacle's Studio.

2/ 3/ 4/ Grabbing frames from video in iMovie is done using export tools.

5/ Frames from interlaced video can appear stripy or jagged when presented in a still image.

6/ Deinterlacing removes the jagged effect but discards half of the image's detail.

7/ Deinterlacing frame grabs is a simple process in Photoshop.

8/ Direct frame export settings in Adobe Premiere Pro.

9/ 10/ Correction of scale may be necessary to compensate for the non-square pixels of DV video.

non-square pixels

Unlike digital photos and graphics, the pixels that compose digital video files are not square. That's why an image 720 x 576 pixels (PAL) or 720 x 480 (NTSC) fits a 4:3 frame. If the frame hasn't been rescaled on export, objects that appeared round on video may look elliptical as a digital photo. Simply rescaling the picture to a correct 4:3 ratio will solve the problem, however, but make sure to scale down, rather than scale up, to preserve the image

sharpness. PAL images should be resized at 720 x 540, and NTSC images should be rescaled to 640 x 480.

interpolating for high resolution

Sometimes there is a need to create very large images from DV files for print. This is often the case with newspapers where the only camera on the scene has been a camcorder. While the limited size of DV frames doesn't lend itself well to printing, there are tools available to help produce more acceptable results.

RedHawk's VideoPics, for example, works as a plug-in for Adobe Premiere, and creates very large images from DV files by pulling information from frames surrounding the one you've chosen for export. The number of neighbouring frames used, and the amount of information they contribute, can

be customised to meet the demands of the individual image, but some excellent results can be had from fairly static footage. Pulling frames from more active or handheld shots can be more tricky, and may result in some blurring or double-exposure effects if you push things too far.

5 the real world

find an audience

Movies are made to be watched. If your production doesn't find an audience it might just as well have not been made. When you're just making movies for your own enjoyment, or for sharing with family and friends, finding viewers isn't too difficult. But when you go it alone as an independent movie-maker, you'll find all sorts of possibilities and hurdles. There's no guarantee that any movie will pull crowds, but you're certainly not short of channels through which to deliver it to viewers.

Keep your options open. If you're working for a client – making corporate or wedding videos – be aware that they might have use for the finished movie in more than one format, be it tape, DVD disc, CD-ROM or even streaming video on the internet. Being versatile with publishing formats will also help reach the widest range of viewers. Even if network TV and multiplex cinemas are beyond your reach, there are still ways to create a buzz around your projects.

freelance professional

DV can take you far beyond the realms of a hobbyist or enthusiast. There are freelance professionals out there using much the same equipment as the amateur and enthusiast. It is not an easy life to get into – a lot of skill and experience are needed – but it can be an exciting and fulfilling one.

ray liffen and intec services

Ray Liffen took the plunge to work as a freelance video-maker long before DV became an affordable format in the mainstream. Ray has 30 years of TV experience behind him, having worked as Studio Resources Manager at the BBC (British Broadcasting Corporation) Television Centre in London. The job requires a good deal of creative and technical problem-solving, and it was only logical that he should be aware of the potential of developing video

technology at the consumer and enthusiast level as well as in the professional broadcast arena. One of his first purchases was a Pioneer PX7 AV processor, which he mainly used for quick video titling. In 1992, Ray bought his first 486 PC, and was soon investigating ways to put it to use for video applications. Some local companies were providing software and cables to use the computer as a controller for linear tape-to-tape editing between professional SVHS

recorders. Sadly, none seemed to work, and Ray instead opted to work with a linear edit controller made by Panasonic and three SVHS decks. His first computer-based non-linear editing system was based around a Miro DC20 capture card. This was an analogue video solution that he used for short sequences and titling, still preferring to use a linear editing set-up for longer projects.

Ray left the BBC in 1996 with the intention of working freelance, based at his home in South London, rather than having to endure long stretches of rush-hour traffic every day. The result was Intec Services, which not only produces work for clients, but provides training for video enthusiasts and troubleshoots problems with video-editing systems.

Towards the end of the 1990s, computers were becoming more powerful, video capture cards were providing better quality (although they were still mainly analogue solutions) and hard drives were getting bigger and faster. In 1997, Ray invested in a FAST AVMaster editing card. While still not working natively in the DV format, the AVMaster provided high-quality video capture via analogue connections, and was one of the first solutions to

5

3

4

a huge bonus, speeding up his workflow and allowing him to take on even more work – which is important, as demand for his services seems to be increasing daily. He is regularly hired to shoot weddings and other family events, but also has a speciality in recording live concerts – for which he uses a remote-controlled multi-camera set-up of his own design! Other typical productions for Ray include university presentations and events such as the annual crowning of the May Queen.

I also hire him as a cameraman on shoots for my own music video company.

As well as video production, Ray is in great demand as an editor for other people's projects, and also for his video duplication service, which includes video standard conversions allowing tapes to be viewed overseas. People are becoming more demanding regarding video, and the prospects for video professionals are extremely strong for anyone with the talent and lateral thinking skills.

! *Find your feet* Ray Liffen isn't an isolated case of a working DV video-maker, but you will find that all the successful freelancers have one thing in common – experience. It is possible to make a living from video production, but don't assume that heavy investment in camcorders and computers automatically qualifies you as a professional video-maker. Don't take money on your first job. Start small and make videos for yourself, for family and your friends. Give yourself time to make mistakes and navigate the many pitfalls of movie-making first-hand without the risk of disappointing paying customers and developing a bad reputation.

provide integrated support for sound and video, rather than relying on the sound card to handle audio. He used this set-up with Adobe Premiere editing software until 2001, when he finally went DV, investing in two Canopus Storm real-time editing cards – still using Adobe Premiere as his editing software. These systems, coupled with his 3CCD camcorders are at the centre of most of Ray's current video work.

According to Ray, working with real-time DV systems has been

6

1-5/ Weddings, music and theatre performances, documentary and sporting events are all staple parts of Ray's working life.

6/ Ray Liffen (left) and the author (bald) on location.

community resources

Even though the prices of camcorders, computers and editing software are lower than some of us ever thought possible, they are still out of reach of many would-be movie-makers. But there are still ways and means to get access to video equipment and training. Many communities now realise the importance of encouraging development in media and visual arts, and there are people out there who want to help you make your movie.

getting going

On leaving school, I started working in retail, on a rather poor wage. I wanted to study film and TV production but had never had the resources of my own with which to build a worthwhile showreel. Living in Edinburgh, Scotland, at the time, I was lucky enough to discover an enterprise called the Video Access Centre. This was a registered charity set up to encourage and promote video production in the city. They had a very limited range of equipment at the time, consisting mainly of two good VHS camcorders and a tape-to-tape linear editing system, but it was enough to get started. Their equipment hire prices were scaled depending on income – meaning that I could make movies, build a showreel, and still afford to eat.

Things developed quickly with the VAC, starting with a second linear editing suite and more camcorders (this time SVHS rather than VHS). Then came bigger premises and 16mm film equipment, at which point the Video Access Centre changed its name to the Film and Video Access Centre. DV Video has also been adopted, with a good selection of 3CCD camcorders, two in-house DV editing systems and a portable editor based around an Apple PowerBook laptop. Twelve years on from when I first joined the centre, it

now has a huge influence on Scottish media production, a new name, Mediabase, and a website: www.edinburghmediabase.com.

Equipment hire is only part of Mediabase's agenda, however. The centre is also well known for running training workshops and seminars on all aspects of movie production. They also have a film-maker in residence, who is available to offer advice and help devise solutions to production problems.

Mediabase's influence on the Scottish movie scene is growing, and the organisation runs a great assortment of projects to screen and promote new talent.

Examples include Blue Room, a monthly showcase of new Mediabase movies at Edinburgh's Cameo cinema; and FortyBight Hours – an annual competition in which competing teams are given only two days to make their movie. Many of Mediabase's schemes are assisted and funded by

organisations such as the Scottish Arts Council, Scottish Screen, and BBC Scotland.

Mediabase is a first-rate organisation, providing a fantastic service – and it is not the only one. The nearby city of Glasgow has its own equivalent in the form of the Glasgow Media Access Centre, claiming to be Scotland's largest. Media resource centres are popping up all over, so get in touch with your local arts council or organisation to find one near you.

! ***Development schemes and grants*** Your local arts council or organisation may also be able to provide information on movie development schemes and grants in your area. These are often competitive programmes that provide funds and support to a small number of short movie projects. Awards are made on the strength of scripts or treatments – and while they are often quite small, they are normally sufficient to make polished productions with professional actors. Very few awards are available, and competition is fierce, so don't bank on winning. But the process of competing can be a great help in pushing projects forward regardless of whether or not you win.

! **Foreign festivals** Cinema-goers are becoming much more responsive to the art and philosophies of other cultures, and you can often find foreign film festivals playing in your nearest city. London and Edinburgh both play host to their own French film festival, for example. If your movie has a message or attitude unique to your own environment, you may find it hugely attractive to overseas' audiences. Dialogue may need to be translated, and subtitles made, but publishing to **DVD** will allow you to create a single master disc with up to 32 subtitle feeds.

film festivals

Film festivals provide the means to have your movies screened in cinemas, and can be a great way to generate publicity around projects and the talent behind them. Hundreds of film festivals take place all over the world, many of which now accept productions shot and mastered using digital video formats.

the circuit

Most countries have their own big film festivals, many of which are happy to take submissions of short movies and digital projects. But space for independent works is often limited, competition is fierce, and big festivals are often overshadowed by the big new feature films – and unless you can get your short movie playing before the premiere of a new Martin Scorsese feature, it's unlikely that anyone will know you were ever there. So while it never hurts to try, I'd suggest that you don't limit your efforts to the mainstream festivals. Keep an eye at what's on offer in the underground. There are many independent film festivals popping up all over the world, from high-profile events like London's Raindance festival, to smaller genre-orientated festivals for horror and sci-fi fans.

In general terms, the film festival circuit is a great way to get exposure for movies, but with audiences being thinly spread across a great many performances, many movie-makers see it more as a means

1

of generating media clippings and reviews that can be used long after the festival has ended. Any positive publicity your movie can generate will help you raise a budget for bigger projects in the future – so aim for as many festivals as possible. The more relevant a festival is to your genre or agenda, the more likely you are to get sympathetic press.

There are some film festivals that go beyond the simple need for exposure and publicity, however. A growing number are being established to showcase work highlighting particular social concerns, or people who are often under-represented in mainstream media. For example, there are at least seven film festivals around the world dedicated to screening movies about human rights issues, and the last time I looked, I counted more than twelve green film festivals. In June, the National Film Theatre in London plays host to the Disability Film Festival, which presents movies made by disabled film-makers. There is also a London Deaf Film Festival, run by the British Deaf Association. The festival's

coordinator, Lucy Franklin told me, 'The festival showcases the work of deaf film-makers and deaf actors from around the world. We attract a 2000-strong audience from the UK and abroad and all screenings are accessible to both deaf and hearing people via BSL/subtitles and voiceover.' The festival is free of charge.

A lot of useful information on film festivals is available online. To find a suitable forum for your movie, take a look at the festivals directory at: www.filmfestivals.com.

1/ 3/ Celebrity appearances can add glamour to bigger festivals, attracting attention to the event and – hopefully – your movie.

2/ An opportunity to gain press and publicity for new works – in this case, with film-maker Stephen Frears.

4/ Festivals often provide the opportunity to attend presentations by established film-makers, such as this workshop by Mike Figgis at London's Raindance Festival.

5/ Film festivals such as the London Deaf Film Festival can provide a platform for people who are under-represented in mainstream media.'

> **!** *Make an impact* People's attention spans are limited – particularly on the net, where there is always a nearby link ready to steal viewers away from you. Short movies have a strong impact online, but the two most important ingredients seem to be simplicity and originality. Unusual and quirky shorts are hugely attractive to office-bound lunchtime surfers – and these are people that start the mass circulation of 'you must see this' emails that turn a fun movie into an online sensation.

movie websites

Broadband internet access is still growing in popularity, and the faster connection speeds are opening more people's eyes to the potential of video delivery on the internet. Web pages are becoming bigger and more dynamic, while internet users are getting hungry for more video-based content.

the way forward

As we've seen in the previous chapter, streaming video technology is still in its infancy, and there is the added drawback that very few mainstream movie companies are happy for anything other than trailers and promotional material to be viewed online. But the current reluctance for mainstream movie giants to enter cyberspace makes it much easier for independent productions to get noticed. Make use of it while you can.

An effective way to get your work seen is to submit it to a movie-orientated website. Two sites at the very forefront are Atom Films (www.atomfilms.com) and iFilm (www.ifilm.com). Both sites host trailers and promotional shorts for mainstream productions, but also feature a wealth of smaller independent productions. Atom Films carries a mixture of live-action video and Flash animation

– the latter becoming popular on the web as it provides a result similar to that of traditional cel animation, sidestepping the need for actors, crew, lights, locations or even a camcorder. iFilm's output is primarily live action.

As with any form of broadcast, there is always a selection process. You have no guarantee that your movie will appear online, but it's well worth a try, as the right movie can receive a lot of attention and work wonders for its makers. Megan O'Neill, director of acquisitions at Atom Films tells me, 'I look for topical shorts, because they tend to be very popular with our audience, many of whom come back on a daily or weekly basis to watch films. One of our most popular shorts is called Star Wars Gangsta Rap – it has had tremendous success on the site. But we also have serious, topical films that do well, like Voice of

the Prophet, which featured a security expert talking about how vulnerable we are to terrorists. He was later killed at the WTC during 9/11. Many topical pieces tend to be flash animations, like SWGR, because they are easier and faster to create. I also acquire comedies, sci-fi shorts, and film festival winners.'

iFilm provides you with the means to add your movie to its website regardless of whether it has been selected – but it will cost you. Think carefully about whether the expense is justified before paying for hosting. But compared to the costs of taking out a streaming media server account and hosting video yourself, iFilm's rates are quite reasonable, and provide a better chance of having the movie seen than if it is only available through your own site.

Edit   View   Favorites   Tools   Help

Back ▾   ●   ✗   ↻   ⌂   🔍 Search   ⭐ Favorites   ● Media   ●   ▾   🖨   W   ▾   ▢   👥   Links   »

  **Because You Like to Watch.**

Help
Send In Film/Video
Dear IFILM...
Video Preferences

 VIES **SHORTS** **TELEVISION** **VIDEO GAMES** **MUSIC VIDEOS** **UNCENSORED!** **BROWSE IFILM** **IFILM Plus+**

SEARCH

New Short Films Straight from Caroline's Comedy Club in Manhattan!

Thursday, September 11

oday on IFILM
ly on IFILM!

PLAY> 200K FREE   **PLAY>** 500K PLUS+   **PLAY>** 56K FREE   **PLAY>** 200K FREE   **PLAY>** 500K PLUS+   **PLAY>** 56K FREE   **PLAY>** 200K FREE   **PLAY>** 500K PLUS+

ney Jr. Sings!
the *Singing Detective*
r, only on IFILM, with
Gibson, Adrien Brody,
e Holmes, more!

Lost in Translation
Exclusive! Bill Murray has
a communication
breakdown with a girl
sent to him as a gift.

***Cabin Fever* Exclusive!**
Locals descend on the
beleaguered inhabitants
of the cabin, and a
bloodbath ensues!

thirteen
Now Playing In Select Theatres

MATCHSTICK **MEN**
OPENS SEPTEMBER **12**

thirteen
now playing in
select theatres

howtimes

er Zipcode GO **OPEN RANGE** **Watch IFILM Commercial-Free**
Click Here FREE 14 DAY TRIAL **IFILM Plus+**

buzz**bin**
Has *Batman 5* been cast?
Find out now.
movies.com

SIC VIDEOS ———————————— [more Music Videos]

PLAY> 200K FREE   **PLAY>** 500K PLUS+

Adema: Unstable
Singer Mark Chavez (half-brother to Korn's Jonathan
Davis) is so strung out over a woman, it feels like he's
sizzling in radioactive fallout.

Top 10 Television

1. Dirty Email Culprit on *The Office*
2. Ah-Nuld for Governor on *Conan*
3. Cocaine Is Addictive
4. Reebok: Terry Tate, Office Linebacker
5. Kids Draw What They Learned on *Conan*
6. Banned PETA Ad: Frisky Cats
7. George W. Bush Talks to Conan
8. Hypothermia on *The Weather*
9. Pam Anderson's Pillow Fight
10. Mean Joe Greene's Famous Coke Ad

ORTS ———————————————————— [more Shorts]

PLAY> 200K FREE

The Last Tape
A CNN reporter gets a ridiculous interview in a secret
cave with an Al-Qaeda operative.

VIES ———————————————————— [more Movies]

PLAY> 200K FREE   **PLAY>** 500K PLUS+

Secondhand Lions Exclusive!
Michael Caine and Robert Duvall talk to IFILM about
their new rough-and-tumble film with Haley Joel
Osment.

EVISION ———————————————————— [more Television]

HBO's *Carnivàle*
Gypsies and charmers scour the land for lost souls;
the series preems Sun., 9/14, 9:30 p.m. ET.

appendix

glossary

Animation
Playback of still images in sequence to give the illusion of movement. Traditionally done by shooting one frame of film at a time and moving the on-screen subject (or artwork) in between shots. Now, much animation is done using computers and 3D modelling software.

Aperture
The opening created by an iris within a camera lens. As the aperture becomes bigger, more light is allowed through to the CCD.

Aspect ratio
The shape of a video frame. Traditional video has a 4:3 aspect ratio, meaning that the picture is four units wide and three units high. Widescreen TV has an aspect ratio of 16:9, and many cinematic movies are wider still.

AVI
Audio Video Interleaved – the most common format for video files on Windows PCs. Many AVI files can also be read on Macs, but as they can use many different methods of compression, there is no single AVI standard for guaranteed playability.

Batch capture
Capture of many logged video clips to a computer in one unattended session.

Bit
The smallest unit of digital information often referred to as ones and zeros. Used to measure memory (eight bits make up a byte) and in reference to colour depth. A greater number of bits per pixel allows a greater number of available colours.

Bitmap
A digital image composed of a mosaic of coloured or greyscale pixels. Bitmap is also the name given to Windows graphics saved in a DIB (Device Independent Bitmap) format with a BMP file extension.

Bitrate
Bitrate (or datarate) is the amount of data that is processed per second in reading or writing a digital media file. DV has a datarate of 3.6 megabytes per second.

Byte
A measurement equating to eight bits. Bytes are used to measure digital files and documents (there are 1,024 bytes to a kilobyte and 1,024 kilobytes to a megabyte). It is also a unit of memory for RAM and hard disks.

CCD
Charge Coupled Device is the light-sensitive chip that converts light from the lens into an electronic signal to be recorded by the camcorder.

CD-ROM
A CD disc containing computer data rather than music.

Chrominance
Colour information in a video signal.

CMYK
Cyan, Magenta, Yellow, and Black. Four colour channels that typically go to make up still images for print. CMYK colourspace does not apply to video.

Codec

Compressor/Decompressor. The instruction set that determines how video is to be compressed into smaller streams. The codec is also necessary for playing the video back, telling the computer how it was compressed in the first place.

Component video (YUV)

Term used to describe the allocation of colour within a video signal, where Y is the luminance (black and white) information, and U and V are colour channels.

Composite video

Relatively low-quality analogue video signal, which passes all colour and luminance information in a single channel. All VHS decks have composite video inputs and outputs.

Compositing

Bringing several video and graphics sources into a single frame so that they seamlessly interact. A typical example is the blue-screen effect where actors are superimposed onto a background that was shot separately.

Compression

Reduction in the size of a digital file. Most commonly used media formats are compressed, be they video, audio or graphics, and most forms of compression are lossy – information is discarded during compression, resulting in an imperfect copy.

Cut

The change from one shot to another without any intermediary effect.

Deinterlacing

Blending the two fields that make up a frame of video to create a single, self-contained image. This is important when preparing video to be viewed on a computer, in a CD-ROM or streaming online.

Device control

Control of a camcorder or VCR's playback functions directly from the computer's editing software. Device control traditionally needed specialised software and professional video decks, but consumer DV devices can be controlled by computers via FireWire.

Disc burning

Copying data (including audio and video) to a recordable disc, such as CD-R, CD-RW, DVD-R or DVD-RW.

Download
Copying files or software from an internet server to be run on your own system.

DV
Digital video – this most commonly refers to Sony's DV and MiniDV video formats.

DVCAM
Sony's professional DV format. Video data is identical to DV, but the tape runs faster and is more robust. DVCAM camcorders tend to have more professional features than their MiniDV counterparts.

DVD
Digital Versatile Disc. A high-capacity disc-based storage format. A DVD can be DVD Video (a popular standard for publishing movies), DVD Audio (for high-definition music), and DVD-ROM for data.

DVD authoring
Publishing movies in DVD Video possibly with interactive menus and other features, such as subtitles, multiple angles, slideshows and audio commentaries.

DVD burner
A computer drive used to copy data to recordable DVD discs.

Edit decision list (EDL)
Log of cuts that compose an edited sequence. An EDL can be used to reassemble movies from source footage long after completion.

Encoding
Conversion of video or audio from one format to another. Preparing video for DVD, for example, requires it to be encoded to MPEG-2 format.

Filter
A video filter is an effect applied to video that alters its appearance. Similarly, physical lens filters are used to control the warmth and tone of light entering a camera lens.

FireWire
Apple's name for the IEEE1394 interface – a port that connects computers to DV camcorders, external drives, scanners, and other data-intensive media devices.

Gigabyte
1,024 megabytes. Hard drives are now measured in gigabytes – large allocations of space for data storage. One gigabyte is required to store just under five minutes of DV footage.

HTML
Hypertext Markup Language. A text-based scripting language used to create interactive websites.

Keying
Identifying certain colours or brightness levels as transparent allowing images to be superimposed one on another.

Interlacing
Division of a video frame into two interlaced fields. PAL video, for example, runs at 50 fields per second, which make up its 25 frames. Pausing an action-packed video on a computer monitor will sometimes allow you to see the jagged edges caused by a time delay between fields.

LCD monitor
The flip-out side screen found on most modern camcorders.

Linear editing
Assembly of video clips in sequence from beginning to end. Mistakes made early in the editing sequence can't be corrected without redoing all subsequent edits.

Luminance
The brightness (or black-and-white) information in a video signal.

Megapixel
One million pixels. A one-megapixel image has a typical size of 1152 x 864 pixels.

MPEG
Motion Pictures Expert Group. MPEG is a method of media compression. MPEG-1 video is the standard used for VideoCDs, while MPEG-2 is used for DVD and digital TV broadcast.

Multimedia
Combination of video, audio and graphics in a single presentation.

Non-linear editing
A method of video editing whereby media can be added or removed from an edit at any time without requiring later cuts to be redone.

NTSC

National Television Standards Committee. TV standard used in the USA, Canada, Japan, and some territories of South America. NTSC-standard DV footage has a frame size of 720 x 480 pixels and a frame rate of 29.97 frames per second.

OHCI

Open Host Controller Interface. A widely accepted standard for computer ports (mainly FireWire and USB), allowing freer and more reliable integration between hardware and software.

PAL

Phase Alternation Line. PAL is the TV standard for the UK, most of mainland Europe, Australia and New Zealand. It is also used in much of Asia. PAL-standard DV footage has a frame size of 720 x 576 pixels and a frame rate of 25 frames per second.

Progressive scan

Video recorded as self-contained frames rather than interlaced fields. Progressive scan video is closer to film in its appearance, but some camcorders sacrifice picture quality when shooting in frame mode.

QuickTime

Apple's Video standard for large uncompressed video and DV files, as well as streaming video and compressed media for CD-ROMs. As with AVI, QuickTime files can be compressed with many different types of codec.

RealMedia

A popular streaming media format for delivery on the internet.

Real-time editing

The ability to preview effects such as transitions and filters without having to render first.

Rendering

Processing video that contains titles, transitions or effects. The process involves remaking footage that contains the effects, which can often require a lot of hard drive space.

RGB

Red, Green, Blue – the term is used to indicate which colour channels are used to compose an image.

Scene detection

Division of video footage into smaller chunks according to changes in the video's date/time information or sudden changes in on-screen content.

S-video (Y/C)
A high-quality analogue video feed, found on SVHS recorders, DV equipment and DVD players. S-video connections split the signal into luminance (Y), and chrominance (C) channels. The S-video signal is of a much higher quality than composite feeds found on standard VHS decks.

Timecode
Numerical labelling of every frame in video footage. Timecode normally refers to hours, minutes, seconds and frames, and is used to create detailed logs for video capture or edit decision lists from the final cut.

VCR
Video Cassette Recorder. A device used to record to, or play back from, video tapes.

Video capture
Transfer of video from tape to a computer-based editing system.

VideoCD
A popular video distribution format in the East. VCD uses MPEG-1 compression to house up to 60 minutes of video on a single CD disc. Feature films normally need to be spread across two discs.

Windows Media Format
Microsoft's streaming media format.

SECAM
The TV standard used for broadcast in France. It relates mainly to TV broadcast, however – DV equipment in France is PAL standard, as with the rest of Europe.

Streaming video
Delivery of video directly on the internet, where media is not stored on the viewer's computer and can't be downloaded. Streaming normally requires specialised servers.

Super VHS
A higher-quality equivalent of VHS video. SVHS cassettes are virtually identical to those of VHS, and SVHS recorders can play and record VHS tapes too.

Super VideoCD
A form of Video CD that uses MPEG-2 video to deliver a higher-quality movie. One SVCD disc can hold around 45 minutes of video, so feature films may need to be spanned over two or three discs.

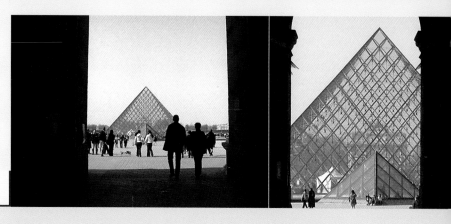

index

credits

John Dollar

John Dollar is, or tries to be, a maker of high-quality TV documentaries with an ethnographic flavour. In the current landscape of TV, he says, such films, and particularly the small independent producers who made them, have disappeared into a hostile wilderness. He takes photos and writes by way of compensation and does so with relish. But while stuck far out in the 'Rub Al Khali of TV commissions' he has occasional delusions that he might better become a tree-surgeon, perhaps, or an itinerant hair-dresser.

Pages 10–11, 40, 42, 44, 49, 68

volcfilm@dircon.co.uk

Ray Liffen

Ray Liffen has been a video professional for over three decades – from working as Studio Resources Manager at BBC Television Centre, to his current freelance work and his own company, Intec Services. Ray enjoys an eclectic range of work. His shoots include corporate and educational productions, wedding videos, and musical performances, and he also provides training for DV newcomers and technical support where it's needed. Ray's diverse (and often heavy) workload is a strong indication of how digital media can work well for those who really know how to use it.

Pages 38, 49, 82, 93, 124, 125

rayliffen@compuserve.com

www.intecservices.co.uk

Mediabase

Edinburgh's Mediabase is a resource and training centre for independent movie-makers. It makes it possible for anyone regardless of income to develop experience and skills in film and video production. There are centres like Mediabase in many big cities – it's well worth tracking them down and signing up.

Pages 126, 127

www.edinburghmediabase.com

Raindance Festival

London's Raindance film festival is dedicated to fostering and promoting independent film in the UK and around the world. It's the focus of many independent movie-makers, and caters for features and shorts, provides a high-profile platform for new talent, and offers training courses and masterclasses to boot.

Pages 128, 129

www.raindance.co.uk

Alison Sweatman

Alison Sweatman has hovered at the fringes of the media industry for many years, not actually making anything but preferring the safety and anonymity that her administrative roles provided. However, frustrated with the creatively dry cocoon that she hung around in, Alison dramatically changed her life in 2002 and left the UK for Nepal. This remarkable kingdom of contrasts inspired her to take a ridiculous number of photographs and shoot her first television documentary. Her love affair with travel continues and other programmes are in development, so she can bring some of the extraordinary lives of others living on this planet into our living rooms.

Pages 41, 54, 66, 69, 73, 80, 132–133

alisonji67@hotmail.com

Unity Pictures

Unity Pictures was responsible for some first-rate promotional videos and adverts, as well as high-impact title sequences for movies. Its work blended excellent photography with ingenious use of computer generated imagery. Many of its images used in this book were created by Hylton Tannenbaum, working for CNN. Unity Pictures has recently ceased trading, but we hope to see more from the company's creative talent in the near future!

Pages 43, 48, 78, 79, 83

Peter Wells

The author, Peter Wells, was trained in film and TV production, and entered the workplace as a microscopic fish in a very big pond. Before long, however, Peter was making a name for himself as deputy editor of the UK's leading (and, at the time, only) desktop video magazine, Computer Video, applying his practical understanding of movie-making to reviews, features and tutorials. Peter now writes freelance, and is still a regular name in Computer Video as well as PC Pro and MacUser. He has had a front-row seat during DV's evolution, and now puts the technology to use with his own music video label, Punkervision Ltd., shooting shows, streaming highlights online, releasing commercial DVDs and making promotional videos for bands. Check out his personal website for up-to-date information on the latest DV developments.

Pages 4–9, 12–13, 19–23, 24, 25, 30–33, 35–43, 45, 47, 48, 50, 51, 55, 56–59, 63, 66, 67, 69–79, 81, 82, 85–91, 94–99, 100–103, 107–109, 112, 113, 115, 118, 119, 120–123, 134–141, 144

www.pcwells.com

Product shots:

A big thanks to all the companies that provided high-quality product shots for this book. They are:

ADS, 65

Advanced Micronics (www.Advanced Micronics.co.uk), 62

AMD, 63

Apple Computer, 61

Beyerdynamic, 52

Canon, 24, 25

Canopus, 65

Compaq, 17

Dazzle, 64

Hercules, 63

HHB, 53, 54

Jessops, 26, 27

JVC, 18, 29, 104, 105

LaCie, 19

Maxtor, 62

Napa, 110

Panasonic, 104, 106

Sennheiser, 52

Sharp, 53

Sony, 14, 15, 16, 23, 64

TDK, 15, 17, 107

acknowledgements

I'd like to say a big thanks to Bob Crabtree for recommending me for this title – and to Nicola Hodgson for taking his suggestion! During the production of the book, Nicola has been a mine of ideas, a pillar of patience, and one of the few people I know who will make a point of reading and understanding alien techie stuff rather than blindly committing it to the page. Nicola's questions, feedback and guidance are hugely appreciated, as is Bruce Aiken's excellent design work, which brings order

to my chaos and – most importantly – makes me look good! Brian Morris' watchful eye ensured I never got away with an easy option, while John Dollar's help in picture research was an absolute blessing.

Speaking of pictures, a mention is due to the Florida band As Friends Rust, who kindly allowed me to use their images on the cover and in the Shoot Everything pages (36–37). Members of AFR are now performing as Salem GVL and you can also buy the DVD that those images came from at www.punkervision.net (am I allowed this shameless plug?).

On a personal level I have to credit my wife, Margaret, for keeping me sane, and my cat, Bucket, for helping me type.